Planning for the Future

Nicholas Martin has played a key role in developing awareness within the voluntary sector of the importance of business planning. In co-operation with NCVO he has run a series of successful seminars and workshops on business planning. Nicholas is a director of MBM Consulting Limited which specialises in working with voluntary organisations. Prior to that he was a policy officer in local government providing advice on contracting, the voluntary sector and employment. Nicholas received an MBA from the London Business School.

Caroline Smith also received her MBA from the London Business School and she co-founded MBM Consulting with Nicholas Martin in 1989. She has worked with voluntary organisations for more than a decade. Originally a development officer and manager in the fields of inner city policy and health and social care Caroline went on to run the Department of Health funded Opportunities for Volunteering scheme based at NCVO.

NCVO – voice of the voluntary sector

NCVO champions the cause of the
voluntary sector. It believes that the
voluntary sector enriches society and
needs to be promoted and supported. It
works to improve its effectiveness,
identify unmet needs and encourage
initiatives to meet them.

Established in 1919 as the
representative body for the voluntary
sector in England, NCVO now gives voice
to some 600 national organisations –
from large 'household name' charities to
small self-help groups involved in all areas
of voluntary and social action. It is also in
touch with thousands of other voluntary
bodies and groups, and has close links
with government departments, local
authorities, the European Community
and the business sector.

Planning for the Future

A Step-by-Step Guide to Business Planning for Voluntary Organisations

Nicholas Martin and Caroline Smith

 NCVO Publications

Published by NCVO Publications

(incorporating Bedford Square Press)

imprint of the National Council for Voluntary Organisations

Regent's Wharf, 8 All Saints Street, London N1 9RL

First published 1993

Typeset by The Word Shop, Bury, Lancashire

Printed in Great Britain by Biddles Ltd, Guildford

A catalogue record for this book is available from the British Library

ISBN 0 7199 1374 8

Contents

List of figures and tables

Figures

Tables

Foreword

People join, work and contribute to charities and other voluntary organisations for a variety of reasons, perhaps seldom considering that only through efficient and effective management can the ultimate aims of those organisations be achieved.

Without clear objectives and careful planning, organisations can fail their donors and clients. Careful attention to the elements of any successful enterprise, such as proper planning, resource allocation, and management ensures that charities and voluntary organisations realise their potential. Otherwise, valuable time and effort can be lost – and the only people who pay for ineffective management of a voluntary organisation are the people or causes it sets out to assist in the first place.

NatWest has long recognised the vital importance of the contribution made by charities and voluntary organisations to society, through our community investment programme. Through this and our extensive banking relationships with charities, we recognise the pressures that charities and voluntary organisations are under to meet increasing demands for their services. We want to make our contribution to helping the voluntary sector to meet this challenge. NatWest's own experience has led us to the view that a critical success factor in any venture is access to sound practical advice; that is why we are pleased to support this publication. Good luck with your business planning.

Martin Gray
Chief Executive, UK Branch Business,
National Westminster Bank

Preface

In the last decade voluntary organisations have experienced many new pressures – the growth of contracting for services, a need to replace statutory funds through fund raising and a growing concern with the monitoring and evaluation of service quality, to name but a few. Voluntary organisations and umbrella bodies such as NCVO have responded to these challenges by providing publications and training. In one key area, that of business planning, the response has, however, been less than complete. While voluntary organisations have increasingly been required to produce business plans there has been no publication aimed at meeting their specific needs as distinct from the needs of private companies. We feel strongly that this is a gap that should be filled.

The need for a guide to business planning

Three main factors lie behind the growth of interest in business planning. Each requires voluntary organisations to be more explicit in specifying their objectives and in detailing how they will be met.

1 Legislation, such as the NHS and Community Care Act 1990, is leading to the development of service contracts and an increasingly formal relationship between funders and voluntary organisations.

2 The government's *Efficiency Scrutiny of Government Funding of the Voluntary Sector*, published in 1990, has raised the profile of accountability and effectiveness on the part of voluntary organisations.

3 The squeeze on statutory funding of the voluntary sector since the late 1980s has forced many organisations to develop strategies for replacing declining sources of funding through marketing and fund raising activity.

The great merit of business planning as a response to these new demands is its comprehensive nature. Rather than looking at budgeting, marketing or any other individual subject in isolation, a business plan considers all aspects of an organisation (finance, staffing, objectives, etc) and the question of how best to co-ordinate them in pursuit of organisational success. Consequently an increasing number of voluntary organisations are concerned to know how they can benefit from the techniques of business planning.

Benefits of business planning

Voluntary organisations can derive many benefits from the application of business planning techniques. At this stage it is worth mentioning just three: (i) A convincing business plan is increasingly becoming a key tool for promoting voluntary organisations to funders. (ii) The process of preparing a plan provides opportunities for strengthening commitment to an organisation's mission and values. (iii) Business plans in a general sense also help voluntary organisations to meet the request of funders and government alike to become more professional.

A conflict with the values of the voluntary sector?

'Does not business planning with its talk of financial forecasts and profit and loss accounts conflict with the values of the voluntary sector and in particular its focus on need and "not-for-profit" status?' A frequently cited objection to business planning is that it is more appropriate for financiers and bankers than the managers of voluntary organisations. The criticism is, in our view, misplaced. This book contends that business planning is in reality a combination of common sense with techniques which can be learnt by voluntary sector workers and funders alike. In many senses business planning represents a more structured approach to what many managers have, in planning their organisations, been doing for some time. Most importantly 'business planning' provides access to a set of tools which empower voluntary organisations and increase the effectiveness with which they pursue their objectives. This book aims, by reference to examples and case histories, to convince even the strongest doubter of the value of business planning to all types of voluntary organisation.

Aims of the book

The main objective of this book is to provide an accessible introduction to the subject and skills of business planning for the trustees and managers of voluntary organisations. The book will also be of value to others – like funders – with an interest in the future development and well-being of the voluntary sector.

There are numerous books on the preparation of business plans and the high street banks often produce helpful guides. These sources of advice, however, tend to concentrate on financial planning and the preparation of sales forecasts. Voluntary sector managers and staff will get little help from these sources in planning the complex 'people' issues, such as the input of volunteers and management committees, which are central to the success of many voluntary organisations. We will discuss these issues alongside material on the application of techniques such as marketing and financial planning to the needs of voluntary organisations.

A recurring theme of this book is that business plans are most useful to voluntary organisations when they become *working tools* – that is when they become constant reference points in resolving problems and identifying priorities. It is important then for voluntary sector workers to develop skills and confidence in business planning. It is through understanding and gaining experience of this process that voluntary organisations can equip themselves for the future.

After completing this book you should have:

- a clear understanding of business planning;

- a practical understanding of how to complete an effective business plan for your organisation; and

- access to a range of management skills and techniques which are of great value to the future prospects of your organisation.

Business planning techniques are already being employed to great effect by many voluntary organisations and this book will contain numerous examples and case histories that illustrate important points.

The organisation of the book

Each chapter starts with a short statement of its learning objectives and describes how the chapter fits within the overall framework of the book. At the end of the chapter a short summary of main points is provided as well as some simple exercises designed to test your understanding of the techniques.

Chapter 1 defines business planning, discusses some of the benefits voluntary organisations can derive from business planning, and outlines the various stages in the process.

Chapter 2 looks at how the business planning process can be started. It covers information needs and answers questions such as who should be involved in preparing the plan.

Chapter 3 considers the importance of setting objectives and identifies the range of areas for which objectives should be set; it also considers the length of time for which the plan is being prepared.

Chapter 4 examines the purpose and benefits to the organisation of collecting and analysing 'marketing' information.

Chapter 5 considers how the organisation might take advantage of opportunities by the means of a promotional or marketing strategy. It discusses the nature of marketing and its value to voluntary organisations.

Chapter 6 discusses the systems all organisations need to ensure that they work effectively. These include systems for management information, monitoring and evaluation, and assuring quality of service.

Chapter 7 discusses the importance of people and personnel systems to the business plan. It looks at planning for staff requirements, management structures and responsibilities, and systems for rewarding and motivating staff.

Chapter 8 provides guidance on the preparation of the financial projections needed for a business plan. It focuses on the inputs and outputs of financial planning and discusses the nature and role of systems of financial reporting.

Chapter 9 introduces and discusses an outline structure for a business plan. It provides extensive advice on how to write the plan and on where to discuss key issues. It also considers the specific needs of different audiences.

Chapter 10 considers the implementation requirements of the business plan. It discusses the content and structure of implementation plans and looks at how to avoid common pitfalls.

Appendix 1 provides suggested answers to exercises in Chapter 8.

Appendix 2 is a short guide for both voluntary sector managers and funders to the evaluation of business plans.

Appendix 3 is an A–Z of widely used business planning terms.

Appendix 4 lists useful addresses and publications where you can find further information.

Appendix 5 gives the names of people whose organisations are featured.

The structure of the book is designed to take you through each important step in preparing an effective business plan. You are recommended to read each chapter and test your understanding by completing the exercises before moving on to the next chapter. This approach will help you understand how different business planning activities relate to each other and will particularly benefit those readers who are new to business planning. Individual chapters can, however, be read on their own by those readers who feel they are relatively experienced in business planning and wish to strengthen their skills in particular areas such as marketing or financial planning.

Acknowledgements

Many people and organisations have contributed directly and indirectly to this book. For sharing their experience of business planning we would like to thank Martin Coleman, Libby Cooper, Trevor Groom, Marc Kiddle, Isobel McConnan, Heather Murison, Louise Pankhurst and Brian Rockcliffe. We would also like to thank those people who attended our business planning workshops at NCVO for their lively contributions and thoughtful questioning.

Chapter 1
Introduction

This chapter sets out the nature and process of business planning and the relevance to, and benefits of, business planning to voluntary organisations.

What is business planning?

In the course of everyday usage many words and concepts take on a wide variety of meanings. *Business planning* is one such concept. To some people it suggests the preparation of financial forecasts; to others business planning is a way of deciding the future direction of an organisation. In practice business planning does involve both these activities and more besides.

A good place to start in the search for such a definition is with the two separate parts of the concept – *business* and *planning*.

Let us begin with planning. It comprises two main activities:

- the preparation of informed estimates about future events; and

- the identification of management actions to influence those events in ways that benefit the organisation and its clients.

Voluntary organisations are highly aware of the effects that legislation and changes in funding policy have on their prospects. Legislation in the field of community care, for example, is radically changing the relationship organisations have with both funders and service users. Voluntary organisations can either be overwhelmed by such change or, by means of planning, can make an organised management response.

The word business is perhaps a bigger obstacle to recognising the relevance of business planning to, say, a group providing accommodation for young homeless people or a day centre for the elderly. The dictionary makes it clear that, while the word 'business' has through common usage become synonymous with commercial activity, it actually refers to any human activity that is organised for a purpose. This purpose may just as well be the provision of services for social benefit as the sale of cars for profit. In effect, all voluntary organisations are themselves 'businesses'.

Let us illustrate this last point with an example of a voluntary organisation providing a service in which the quality of the *personal* as opposed to the *business* relationship between the organisation and the user is of central importance. The Bromley Alcohol Advisory Service (BAAS), which produced its first business plan in 1990, is an alcohol counselling and advice service in southeast London. It provides individual counselling for up to 200 local people and has over 20 volunteer counsellors as well as 2 full-time staff who are available for counselling work. In what sense is it a business as defined above?

1 It has a clear organisational purpose – the prevention of serious problems of alcohol abuse through community-based services – which requires well organised management activity.

2 BAAS has several funders to whom it must communicate a sense of direction if it is to continue 'in business'.

3 It has a responsibility to consider how all aspects of the organisation – promotion, premises, staff training, etc – encourage the attendance and recovery of people from all backgrounds.

In short the organisation of BAAS is at least as complex as any private business.

To manage successfully and cope with their changing environment voluntary organisations must anticipate and prepare for events that will influence their future. And in meeting these challenges voluntary organisations are employing the same skills and techniques such as budgeting, marketing and personnel management as their counterparts in the private sector.

Business planning then is defined by two concepts:

- *planning* the preparation of informed estimates about future events and of management action to influence those events; and

- *business* the organisation of purposeful human activity.

A comparison of the nature and scope of business planning with another form of planning – *strategic planning* – will further clarify the definition of business planning given above. The two types of planning differ in three important respects:

1 *Focus* A strategic plan seeks answers to questions such as 'Where do we want the organisation to be in five years' time?' and 'What is the organisation's mission?' Business planning focuses on the activities, systems and skills required to achieve objectives that reflect the mission.

2 *Timescale* Business plans are usually prepared for a shorter timescale (from one to three years) than a strategic plan which can be for periods of five years or more.

3 *Process* Business planning, as this book will demonstrate, is a continuous process with detailed plans subjected to routine monitoring and review. Strategic planning, on the other hand, is an activity like setting the overall mission that takes place only periodically.

Business planning, therefore, is the activity of preparing an organisation for events that will influence its future. It involves detailed consideration of all the factors (people, organisational systems and structures) that will contribute to successful performance. And it is a continuous activity based on regular monitoring and review. In short business planning is an essential activity for any organisation.

Benefits of business planning

Table 1 provides a snapshot of the benefits voluntary organisations have realised as a result of preparing a business plan. It illustrates the wide range of potential benefits, from improved financial planning to improved service delivery.

Table I   The Benefits of Business Planning

Benefit	Illustration of benefit
Highlight the needs of users and how best to meet those needs	A charity matching health workers interested in working overseas with development agencies gained an improved understanding of the recruitment needs of their clients.
Improve the quality of service	Modernising the production process of a journal enabled a national voluntary organisation to provide information when it was needed by subscribers.
Identify new needs or markets to be served	An organisation was able to research the needs of organisations in other parts of the country and to adjust its services to win new sources of finance.
Gain a better understanding of the organisation's financial structure	An organisation was able to see more clearly which of its income generation activities were making the largest financial contribution to supporting other activities.
Promote the organisation to users and funders	An evaluation agency used its plan to assist it in applying for renewal of existing funding and to demonstrate its achievements to potential funders.

Benefit	*Illustration of benefit*
Identify the support systems necessary to realise organisational objectives	A charity recognised the need for new financial systems to help monitor its growing range of activities.
Assist with the process of making priorities	On the basis of a survey of user needs a charity put additional staff resources into a key service.

The benefits of business planning to voluntary organisations can be further illustrated in respect of two themes: coping with chance events and managing growth.

A part is played in the life of all organisations by chance events – cheaper premises become available unexpectedly or the director learns of a new source of funding while attending a seminar, for example. While it is not possible to plan for all such events, chance does tend to favour those organisations who have prepared to take advantage of opportunities and are aware of potential threats. A business plan is one of the best forms of such preparation.

A business plan can also make an important contribution to the management of growth; each stage in the growth of an organisation gives rise to new needs and a business plan can help the organisation prepare to meet them. At the start-up stage, for example, the plan will focus on demonstrating the need for the service and on detailing the personal and financial resources necessary to get the organisation established. As the organisation becomes more securely established the plan will focus more closely on those factors, such as service quality, that will make the organisation a success. The plan will also need to identify how the organisation will secure the balance of staff skills necessary for the expansion and consolidation of its activities.

A model of the business planning process

Figure 1 illustrates the wide range of activities that make up business planning. It is this consideration of all the aspects of an organisation

Figure I   The Business Planning Process

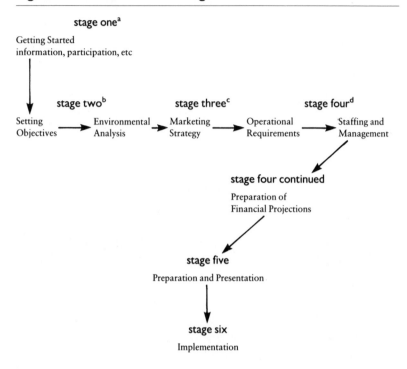

stage one[a]

Getting Started
information, participation, etc

stage two[b]   **stage three**[c]   **stage four**[d]

Setting → Environmental → Marketing → Operational → Staffing and
Objectives   Analysis   Strategy   Requirements   Management

stage four continued

Preparation of
Financial Projections

stage five

Preparation and Presentation

stage six

Implementation

Notes:
a   Includes resolving questions such as who is involved in preparing the plan.
b   Environmental analysis includes looking at the current conditions, eg
    finance, staffing, facing the organisation.
c   The preparation of a strategy to assist the organisation make the most of
    opportunities identified in the environmental analysis.
d   Includes the identification of systems that will be essential for successful
    implementation of the plan.

and of how they are integrated that makes a business plan such a
valuable resource. The apparent separation of the activities in the
diagram does not, however, fully represent the reality of the process.
In many instances activities such as marketing and financial forecast-
ing will be taking place in tandem rather than separately, and there

will be a constant feedback from the 'later' to the 'earlier' phases of the process.

Summing up

Business planning is essentially the activity of preparing an organisation for events that will influence its future. It is an activity that involves detailed consideration of all the factors that contribute to successful performance and it is a continuous activity in which monitoring and review play an important part. We have seen that business planning can bring numerous benefits to all organisations and that the complex environment faced by voluntary organisations is increasing the relevance to them of business planning techniques.

The process of business planning is wide-ranging. The business planner begins by identifying information needs and then moves through a series of stages which result ultimately in the preparation and implementation of the business plan.

Chapter 2
Getting Started

This chapter sets out the key steps to take before embarking on business planning activity and details the information necessary to prepare a business plan. It also describes some typical problems of business planning and how these can best be avoided. It also clarifies the potential role for outside advisers in the preparation of a plan for your organisation.

There are many ways in which voluntary organisations first become involved in business planning:

1   A business plan may be required by an important funder. The Child Accident Prevention Trust, a national voluntary organisation working in the field of child safety, was, for example, committed to providing the Department of Health with a plan as part of its grant conditions.

2   A plan may be needed to assist the organisation replace declining sources of funding. In the case of the Disability Resource Team, a London-based organisation offering disability training, a business plan was needed to detail how the organisation could broaden its funding base.

3   A plan may also be needed to guide the future direction of the organisation and to indicate the management actions that will be necessary to ensure success. This was true in the case of Charities

Evaluation Services, a national organisation which promotes self-evaluation by voluntary organisations.

However an organisation arrives at the point where it needs to start the business planning process, there are a number of steps to take before getting involved in the detail which will save time and reduce the likelihood of problems when you come to implement your plan. You will need to consider the following:

- the information required to complete the plan;

- the basis.on which staff and other 'stakeholders' will be involved in preparing the plan;

- the principal reason for producing a business plan and how this will be communicated to interested parties;

- the problems likely to be encountered during the planning process and the range of solutions open;

- whether outside advice or assistance is required; and

- what is a realistic timescale for completing the business plan.

Information needs

In preparing the business plan you will need to have access to accurate information on many subjects. You should attempt to answer as many of the questions as possible in the information needs checklist before you start to prepare a business plan.

Information needs checklist

Aims and objectives

Does the organisation have a clear set of aims and objectives?

Where are they written?

Are they likely to need any revision during the planning process?

If revision is needed, how will it be organised?

Distinctive strengths

What makes it likely that your organisation will succeed in achieving its objectives?

Why should users and funders regard your organisation as attractive to support?

Services

What services does your organisation currently provide?

How many people use those services?

What are the views of service users and funders on your current services?

Is there a need to modify existing services or to introduce new services?

Users

Who are the intended users of your services?

Is the organisation successful in reaching its target user groups?

Are the needs of your users changing in any way?

Marketing information

What external factors, such as government legislation or changes in funding programmes, are likely to have an effect on your organisation?

What information do you have on the activities of organisations with objectives and services similar to those of your own?

What information do you have on best practice in your organisation's areas of service?

Funders and purchasers

Who are your current funders?

What are the terms of the funding agreements with these funders, eg amounts of money, expiry dates, etc?

Are funding priorities changing?

Is funding likely to continue?

Are funders likely to shift towards service contracts?

What alternative sources of funding are available to your organisation?

Management systems

What management systems, eg financial, monitoring and evaluation, etc does your organisation have?

What information do you have on the strengths and weaknesses of these systems?

Staffing and management

What is the current staffing and management structure of your organisation?

Do you know whether this structure is working effectively?

What are the current terms and conditions and job descriptions of staff?

Are these likely to change?

Are there any significant personnel issues which need resolving?

Finances

What is the latest information you have on the financial status of the organisation?

What financial resources do you currently have?

Are any significant changes in your finances likely, eg is a cost such as rent likely to change in any significant way?

Do you anticipate any cash or other financial crisis in the future?

Legal issues

Are there any significant legal issues on which you will need advice, eg on managing a contract?

Premises

Are your current premises suitable for your needs?

Are your needs likely to change?

If they are, how easily can you leave your current premises and find a new location?

Equipment

What is the current condition of equipment used by your organisation?

Will it need repair or replacement in the near future?

Image and reputation

What image and reputation does your organisation have with users, funders and other organisations?

What image and reputation would you like?

It is likely that you will already have the information to answer many of these questions. Running through the checklist is, however, likely to result in the identification of a number of gaps in the information you need for your business plan. It is essential that you list these gaps and identify how you plan to fill them. You should identify the people responsible for collecting the information and the collection deadline. As long as you have a clear plan for assembling this information you should not worry if collection overlaps other business planning activities.

Involving staff and other 'stakeholders'

A common problem in implementing a business plan is that staff and other 'stakeholders', such as management committee members, are unhappy with the content of the plan because they were not involved in its preparation. In order to anticipate such problems it is advisable to set out clearly the basis on which different people will be involved in the planning process.

Essentially you may decide between two main options – involvement of a wide group of interested people or the restriction of involvement to a limited few. The pros and cons of the two options are set out in Table 2.

Table 2   Involvement in the Business Planning Process

Option	Pros	Cons
'Wide'	Builds ownership of the plan	Danger that the planning process is slowed down
	Reduces possibility of conflict about proposals	Possible loss of clarity in the plan if too many people are involved
'Narrow'	Responsibility for preparing plan is clear – reduces delays	Increased potential for conflict over the plan and its implementation

The choice between the two options must depend on the circumstances of your own organisation. If your organisation is small and normally involves everyone in decision-making, then it would be advisable to involve as many people as possible. If, however, your organisation is relatively large and there is an expectation that management will lead on strategic issues such as planning, then the narrow model will be more suitable.

The purpose of a business plan

If you are clear about your reasons for preparing a business plan and can communicate this to interested people within your organisation, then you will reduce the likelihood that staff and others will feel threatened by the plan. For example, if staff are not informed about the purpose and timescale of the plan, and see a selected few disappear into closed rooms to develop it, then the likelihood of disaffection is high. If, however, you communicate the reasons for preparing a plan, and identify channels for individuals to find out more about it, then your chances of getting support for the end-product will almost certainly be improved.

Using outside advisers

The preparation of the business plan involves a wide range of skills and techniques and you may feel, especially if you are producing a plan for the first time, that the support of an adviser or consultant would be helpful. There are several possible reasons for seeking professional assistance:

- access to specialist skills not available within the organisation, eg finance or marketing;

- lack of time to produce the plan internally and the ability to earmark the resources to pay for outside help;

- judgement that a fresh or 'objective' assessment of the organisation would be valuable; or

- belief that a consultant is more likely to identify answers to the needs of the organisation

The involvement of an adviser or consultant may not be appropriate if:

1　It is essential to learn about business planning by preparing the business plan internally.

2　The skills needed to prepare the plan are present within the organisation or can be acquired from volunteers or members of your management committee.

3　The involvement of an outside 'expert' would be likely to reduce the sense of ownership of the plan by staff and others.

You may well conclude that while you do not need a consultant to prepare the full business plan, the participation of an adviser in certain activities might be beneficial. A consortium of disability organisations, for example, used a consultant to help it to resolve differences about organisational objectives that were inhibiting progress in the development of a plan.

If you do decide to involve an outside adviser in the preparation of your business plan then it is important that you obtain as much benefit from the arrangement as possible. You should ensure that:

1　Any consultant appointed has experience of working with voluntary organisations in the preparation of business plans. Various lists of suitable advisers are kept, eg by the Management Development Team at NCVO. You should also take up references supplied by prospective consultants.

2　Terms of reference are agreed with the consultant that are clear about the support required and detail what is expected in terms of written reports, completion dates and costs.

3　A consultant is appointed who will collaborate in the preparation of the plan rather than simply present one based on his or her conclusions. If you can work well with the consultant you are more likely to improve your own skills and confidence in business planning.

Anticipating 'problems'

It is very likely that, however well you prepare, you will encounter problems in producing your business plan. Table 3 identifies some very common problems and possible responses. In general, the more you anticipate problems and prepare your response the less likely it is that the planning process will be delayed.

Table 3   Planning Problems and Management Responses

Problem	Possible response
Lack of time to plan	Project team to give extra impetus Employ outside adviser or consultant
Non-co-operation of key people	Mechanisms for involvement Strong management lead
Difficulties in collecting information	Set realistic timetables Concentrate on essential items of information
Conflict over plan content	Forums to bring out and resolve conflicts Strong management lead

The overall management of the business planning process will be helped if a clear and realistic timetable for completion is specified. The length of the process will depend on the circumstances of each individual organisation. For example, if the organisation has a wide range of activities or wishes to conduct extensive research among current and potential users of its services, then the planning process will be relatively long. If, on the other hand, the organisation is small, has only a few services and a simple management structure, then a business plan can be put together fairly quickly.

What is clear is that there should be a timetable for preparing the plan. This should

- detail the different stages of the planning process, indicating who will be responsible for each stage and the dates by which each stage will be completed; and

- specify dates for a draft business plan, for consultation on the draft, and for approval of the final version of the plan.

A strategic plan first?

Many organisations have strategic plans for periods of, say, three to five years and then develop a series of business plans which detail how the longer-term strategy will be achieved. This enables these organisations to relate their business plans to a longer-term understanding of what the organisation wishes to achieve.

Although there are some advantages to preparing a strategic plan before the business plan, an effective and useful business plan can be prepared without a strategic plan. As long as your organisation has a sense of what it wishes to achieve, and is able to translate this into clear objectives, then it is in a good position to prepare a business plan. In the next chapter we move on to discuss the setting of objectives.

Summing up

Before involving yourself in the detailed organisation of a business plan it is advisable to take a number of steps in preparation. Doing so will save time at a later stage of the business planning process. It is particularly important to prepare a checklist of the information you will need and to anticipate how you will manage problems that often occur when preparing a business plan.

Exercises

I   Spend about 30 minutes reviewing the information checklist. What are the most important gaps in the information your organisation needs? List the ways in which you intend to fill the information gaps?

2   In respect of your own organisation, evaluate the two options (given in Table 2) for involving stakeholders in the planning process. Who are you going to involve? Why?

3   What problems do you anticipate facing in preparing your business plan? Make a short list of the ways in which you intend to respond to each problem.

Chapter 3
Setting Objectives

This chapter sets out the importance of setting clear objectives. It describes the procedures involved, the areas for which objectives should be set, and the need to set realistic timescales for achieving objectives.

The importance of setting objectives

Objectives are essentially the aims towards which your activity is directed. They describe what you wish to achieve by joining together and organising. There are several reasons why it is essential that your business plan is based on a clear set of objectives:

1 A clear set of objectives will guide and structure the rest of the business planning process. It is very difficult to plan services and identify staffing needs without an understanding of the results you wish to achieve.

2 Without a clear sense of direction, staff and volunteers will be unsure about their roles and will soon become demoralised. A set of objectives is, therefore, an important way to build commitment to the aims and activities of your organisation.

3 The implementation of your business plan will be helped if those responsible for implementation have a clear understanding of the main aims of the plan.

A voluntary organisation without a clear set of objectives will soon become trapped in a vicious circle in which the absence of agreed objectives demoralises key people and in turn leads to further confusion about the organisation's goals. This circle will need to be broken before the organisation begins to collapse. The problems associated with the failure to specify objectives are illustrated in the case study on 'Setting Objectives'. In this case the organisation was able eventually to define its objectives and proceed to implement its business plan.

Case study – setting objectives

Workable

Workable is a consortium of 11 local and national organisations with expertise in the employment of people with disabilities. Its members include large national organisations like MENCAP and smaller local organisations like the Disability Resource Team. The organisation was formed in 1990 in order to facilitate joint working which would increase employment and training opportunities.

Workable employs two staff, a director and an assistant, and provides a range of services including advice and information to employers who are interested in employing more disabled people. Although Workable's business plan did describe the overall purpose of the organisation it did not detail either the objectives or the means by which objectives would be pursued. A particularly difficult issue for members was the means by which Workable could be involved in projects with private sector employers aimed at training and employing disabled people. Understandably many members felt that Workable might end up doing work that should be done by the members themselves.

The lack of direction made it hard for staff to develop services and was beginning to threaten the existence of the organisation. As the chair of Workable observed, 'There was a clear commitment to the concept of the organisation but we all felt we were falling short in setting manageable objectives that would ensure its future survival.'

In response to these difficulties the Board of Workable invited a consultant to interview the member organisations on their views about Workable's future direction. The consultant concluded that a common set of objectives could be identified and that Workable's role in projects should be defined as that of co-ordination. On the basis of the consultant's report the director was able to make a series of proposals to the Board which resulted in agreement on the principal objectives of Workable. In addition the Board was able to provide the director with guidance on service priorities. Heather Murison, the director of Workable, concluded, 'It was vital to go through this process in order to secure the direction and future of Workable.'

Procedures for setting objectives

It may well be that your organisation's objectives were clearly defined when it was set up and that no amendment is required for the business plan. Equally, as we saw in the case of Workable, your objectives may need to be clarified or written for the first time. There are three main ways in which to set about this task:

1 Establish a forum for discussing the future direction and objectives of your organisation. This could involve members of staff, the management committee and volunteers, and could take the form of a day away from the office and its pressures. If you do take this option make sure that you set a clear agenda for the discussion and that you nominate someone to write up the conclusions of the discussion.

2 Invite interested people such as staff and management committee members to answer questions on their vision for the organisation. You could do this yourself or, as in the case of Workable, invite an outsider to facilitate the process.

21

3 Prepare a report on your organisation's objectives and then consult with others about its recommendations. The report should be prepared by someone with authority in the organisation – a senior member of staff or member of the management committee.

The potential difficulties of setting objectives should not be underestimated. Since objectives reflect the very reasons for an organisation's existence they are a major area for personal disagreement. It can also be very difficult to be precise in the way in which you formulate objectives. The following guidance points will help.

1 In selecting a procedure to set objectives balance the need for ownership, which is promoted by away days and consultation, with the need for objectivity. The latter may require outside advice or leadership from senior management.

2 Make sure that the process is a structured one. Avoid lengthy wrangles over the content of objectives and set a deadline for reaching agreement.

The organisation's objectives

There are many areas for which objectives must be set. These should include:

- *service range* – the types of service or activity which you will provide;

- *target users* – the groups and numbers of people or organisations to whom you plan to provide a service, eg people with learning difficulties, social service departments, etc;

- *intended benefits* – the benefits that users will receive from your services, eg development of skills, improved quality of life, etc;

- *service outcomes* – the results of providing a service; and

- *other features* – including the development of distinctive skills and experience among staff, and the image and reputation of the organisation.

Table 4 illustrates how an alcohol counselling agency specified its objectives in each of these areas. It shows how the agency has detailed how it intends to apply its overall purpose in specific objectives. For example, it intends to achieve its goals of reducing alcohol misuse by a mix of individual, group and family therapy. The agency is clear about the benefits it intends for its clients and it declares objectives in terms of the numbers of people it plans to help. As indicated above, setting objectives in this way will structure and guide the rest of the business planning process. For example:

1   The definition of target users will help the agency decide what promotional activity it should take to reach each client group.

2   Specifying the number of clients has clear implications for the management and staffing of the agency, and for the accommodation the agency occupies.

3   The identification of service outcomes indicates the areas in which measures of service impact will need to be developed.

4   By specifying clear and comprehensive objectives the financial needs of the agency are clearly defined.

The conclusion is that unless you document a clear set of objectives many of the subsequent business planning activities will essentially take place in the dark. The chance that your plan will be coherent and integrated will be greatly reduced.

The next steps

Once your objectives are outlined as illustrated in Table 4, translate them into a form that makes action possible:

1   Set goals or targets in respect of each objective.

2   List the tasks that will be undertaken in order to achieve these targets.

3   Identify timescales and responsibility for each target and the related tasks.

Table 4 Objectives: Alcohol Counselling Agency

Overall purpose or mission: to help reduce the misuse of alcohol and the consequent health, social and economic problems

Service range	Target users	Numbers	Benefits	Service outcomes	Other features
Individual counselling	Problem drinkers and their partners, families, and significant others	600 individual sessions	Alleviation of problems	Changed drinking behaviour	Enhanced status with purchasers of services
Group sessions	A representative mix of local community	5 weekly groups	Assistance in coping with alcohol dependence and its consequences	Continued flow of referrals	High profile in district
Family work		Work with 10 families		Positive client feedback	

Table 5 Objectives: Setting Targets and Tasks

Objective	Targets	Tasks	Responsibility
Provision of individual counselling sessions	450 sessions in year one	Recruit 2 counsellors and 5 volunteers	Director, senior counsellor, education worker, management committee
		Prepare two rooms for counselling	
		Promotional material to GPs, social services and probation service	
	600 sessions in year two	Recruit third counsellor	As above
		Prepare additional counselling facilities	
		Extend promotion to police service	
		Outreach work with local community groups	

Table 5 illustrates this activity for one of the objectives of the alcohol counselling agency we discussed earlier.

You should prepare a similar table for each of the objectives of your organisation. Not only will this help you prepare the rest of the business plan but it will provide you with guidelines against which to assess your progress in implementing the plan.

Distinctive capabilities of the organisation

As part of the process of setting objectives and targets for your organisation you should spend some time thinking about your organisation's 'distinctive capabilities'. These capabilities are the particular attributes of your organisation that you believe make it likely that you will achieve your objectives and targets. It may be that your distinctive strength is the quality and experience of your staff and volunteers. Or it may be that users are highly satisfied with the services you offer. Identifying your organisation's distinctive capabilities will have a number of benefits. It will give readers of your business plan a clear picture of why you are likely to succeed. It will influence funders who are considering whether to invest in your organisation. And it will help you prepare an analysis of your organisation's strengths and weaknesses (see Chapter 4).

Setting realistic timescales

It is important that you set realistic timescales for the realisation of your objectives. If you are over ambitious in setting timetables you will place yourself and staff under excessive pressure, and may feel that you are failing as an organisation. The first check against over ambition is your analysis of the tasks actually required to achieve the targets you have set. Ask yourself

- whether you are likely to have sufficient time and resources to complete the tasks in the proposed time; and

- whether additional resources can be found to complete these tasks within the timetable.

If the answer to both these questions is no, then amend the targets you have set so that they accord with the time and resources available to your organisation.

A second check is to make explicit the assumptions on which your analysis of targets and timescales is based. These assumptions may include

- the timing and availability of grant funding;

- the time it will take to recruit and train key staff;

- the effectiveness of your promotion in reaching target groups of user; and

- estimates of the cost of important items such as rent and rates.

Each of these assumptions should be critically assessed and the effect on your timetable of changes in assumptions should be analysed and discussed. This process of reviewing and amending assumptions is known as sensitivity analysis and it is a valuable business planning technique. Ultimately, however, you will need to use your judgement about what constitutes a realistic timescale for achieving objectives and avoid succumbing to outside pressures to agree impossible deadlines.

In Chapter 1 we noted that business plans were typically prepared for shorter time periods than strategic plans (see p. 3). It is not possible to say precisely how long the planning period should be since the environment faced by voluntary organisations is so uncertain. A business plan can be for as little as one year or as long as three years. A plan for a period of more than three years is unlikely to be of much value to your organisation since the assumptions upon which it is based will be subject to too much change.

A sensible compromise would be a two-year rolling business plan in which you review your plan at the end of its first year and produce a revised plan for the subsequent two years. This plan would in its turn be reviewed after a further year. Make sure that when you set your objectives that the time period for the plan is clear.

Summing up

The setting of clear objectives provides a foundation for the rest of your business plan. The objectives you set for your organisation should encompass services, intended users, and the results you hope to achieve. A detailed set of targets and tasks should be prepared on the basis of your objectives, and realistic timescales for the achievement of objectives must be agreed.

Exercises

1 Ask some colleagues to write down what they think are the five main objectives of your organisation. Then compare results. Are you and your colleagues in agreement about objectives? How do these views compare with the 'official' objectives of the organisation that are set down in annual reports etc?

2 Prepare a summary of your organisation's objectives using both the headings in Table 4 and any others that you think are appropriate.

3 On the basis of the summary of your objectives, identify targets you wish to achieve and when you wish to achieve them.

4 On what assumptions was your answer to Exercise 3 based? Treat these assumptions to a sensitivity analysis. How does this analysis affect key targets?

Chapter 4
Collecting and Analysing
Marketing Information

This chapter explains why it is important to collect marketing information by means of an environmental analysis, what preparing an environmental analysis entails, the types and ways of collecting information necessary for the business plan and how to interpret and present the findings.

By setting objectives for your organisation you will have given the rest of the business planning process a firm foundation. We now need to consider how you can demonstrate the credibility of those objectives by the collection and analysis of marketing information.

Environmental analysis

An environmental analysis is essentially the investigation and analysis of the world in which your organisation is functioning. This includes consideration of the effect on your organisation of government legislation, user needs, funding policies and the activities of other organisations. For example, thousands of voluntary organisations are being affected by the introduction, as a result of legislation, of community care. In turn community care has implications for funding mechanisms and is leading to the introduction of contracts and service level agreements in the place of grants.

There are numerous reasons why it is important to prepare an environmental analysis for your organisation:

1   It will help you understand the needs of the users of your organisation's services. Voluntary Service Overseas (VSO) has been considering the setting up of a residential training centre for volunteers. Realising that it would have spare places in the centre, VSO conducted research among other voluntary organisations into their criteria for buying residential training facilities.

2   It will help you identify ways in which your organisation can better meet the needs of its users. VSO's research revealed, for example, that it would need to offer single bedrooms if it were to attract organisations to its centre.

3   It will also help you identify the needs of potential new users of your organisation. The Disability Resource Team (DRT) conducted a major postal and telephone survey of potential subscribers to its services. It was able to collect vital information from potential users of the services offered by DRT and to evaluate the likely response to the offer of new service packages.

4   It will help you assess the image and reputation of your organisation. Information on the assessment by users of your strengths and weaknesses is particularly useful. The International Health Exchange (IHE), which manages a register of health professionals with an interest in working overseas, found that one-third of the development charities which used the service were unclear about how the service worked. IHE were able to respond with a new leaflet giving clear information on the service.

5   It will help you understand how potential users find out about the services they need and how important factors, such as the location of your premises, are in their decision to contact your organisation. An audience survey used by a community theatre included questions on the sources of information used by the audience to find out about plays.

6 It will help you learn about activities of organisations similar to your own and to establish what is regarded as 'best practice' in your field.

7 It will help you establish the credibility of the ideas for service development you have set out in your objectives. DRT was, for example, able to measure interest in its service packages and to modify their content accordingly.

The many advantages of completing an environmental analysis boil down to the essential benefit of an improved understanding of:

● the opportunities available to your organisation, eg to gain new users, to introduce new services, to win extra funding, etc; and

● the threats posed to your organisation by events in its environment, eg by changing funding policy, by the emergence of other organisations with aims similar to your own, etc.

Without this understanding your business plan will be adrift from the actual conditions in which your organisation works.

Key questions

Before starting your environmental analysis you need to answer three key questions:

I What are your main reasons for wishing to collect marketing information? Your answer to this question will directly influence the type of information you need to gather and the collection methods you choose.

2 What information do you already have? Many organisations underestimate the extent to which they already have much of the information they need.

3 What information gaps do you need to fill?

To illustrate how you might prepare an environmental analysis for your own organisation consider the experience of two entirely separate voluntary organisations: Language Line, an innovative telephone interpreting service based in East London, and a small group of refugees who sought to investigate the feasibility of an interpreters' co-operative. We shall consider how the organisations defined the principal purpose of their research, how they identified the types of information they needed, and the collection methods they chose to use.

Completing an environmental analysis

Case studies – The purpose of an environmental analysis

Language Line

Language Line was set up in January 1990 to provide a telephone interpreting service in seven minority ethnic languages. Remarkably, as director Marc Kiddle observed, 'although similar services were long established in Australia, the United States and Holland, this was the first telephone interpreting service in Britain. It was, then, truly innovative.' At the outset, however, Language Line did not know of the existence of similar services and so it had nowhere to turn for advice or experience. The initial objective was to offer the service to health organisations in the Tower Hamlets area of London with plans to extend the scheme to other users and areas.

The project received initial support for a pilot from a government task force, British Telecom and a charitable trust. The pilot was judged a success and in early 1991 it was decided that research would be necessary to establish whether the project could find alternative sources of income when the initial grants ended. An analysis would, therefore, be needed of the interest of potential users.

Interpreters' Co-operative

A group of recently arrived refugees were interested in establishing a face-to-face interpreting service. The local council gave them a small grant for a feasibility study and identified a local consultant to assist them. Was there a need among local professionals for such a service? If there was, could this group meet the need, and would people be willing to pay for the service?

Types of information

There are five main types of information that you may want to collect as part of your environmental analysis. These are

- information on the needs and opinions of current and potential users of the services of your organisation. The views of past users of the service will also be valuable in assessing your strengths and weaknesses.

- Information on important trends and influences in the organisation's environment;

- the criteria used by grant makers and other funders in deciding whether to support funding applications;

- existing patterns of service in areas of activity that you wish to become involved; and

- the activities of organisations with similar services to those of your own.

The precise nature of the information needed will also be influenced by the information available and the remaining gaps. These considerations were critical for our case study organisations.

Case studies – information needs

Language Line

The director of Language Line and its five permament interpreters knew that there had been a steady increase in demand from existing users. They believed, from discussion with local officials, that the separation of purchaser and provider roles, as a result of reforms of the health service, was leading to a new emphasis on access to services for minority language speakers. They also knew that there were other concentrations of minority language speakers who made demands on the statutory services, eg police force, health service, etc that might become users.

In other areas, however, the staff were largely in the dark. Until 1991 the service had been provided free – would new customers be willing to pay for the service? What were their decision-making procedures? The staff were not aware of any direct competitors and did not know how successful their limited public relations activity had been in creating awareness of Language Line.

On the basis of this assessment of information gaps the project decided it needed to develop information on the following:

- existing provision of interpreting services for minority language speakers (if any) by potential purchasers;

- plans of potential users for improvements in interpreting services;

- the decision-making procedures of potential new users; and

- the awareness potential users had of Language Line and their interest in its services.

Interpreters' Co-operative

The group of refugees felt confident that there was a need for the service they proposed. Home Office figures showed that nearly 4,000 refugees had arrived in Britain from their country in the last six months, adding to an already resident population of 6,000. The overwhelming majority of this community could not speak English and, as a result, the statutory services were struggling to cope. Although voluntary and community groups had attempted to respond, our group of interpreters knew that they too were being overwhelmed.

It was far less clear to the group whether there were any resources to pay for such a service. Were grants available from statutory services or charitable trusts? Would health authorities or solicitors' practices be willing to buy interpreting services on a commercial basis? The group was also interested to know whether potential users would require them to acquire a recognised interpreting qualification before offering financial support.

Having reviewed the information already available the group decided on the following information objectives:

- the collection of all available information on the size of the minority language group;

- the identification of any services similar to that proposed by the group and the funding structure of those services;

- the details of current interpreting provision for the particular language group of the refugees;

- the availability of resources to support a new service; and

- the level of interest among potential users in a new interpreting service.

Information collection: methods and sources

There are three main sources of the information needed to complete the environmental analysis:

- internal sources of information

- 'secondary' or desk research

- 'primary' or field research

The definitions of each of these information sources, the range of methods of information collection they give rise to, and some of the advantages and disadvantages associated with each source are discussed below.

In voluntary organisations where resources are likely to be limited it is essential to make the most of the *internal sources* of information. It is almost certain that more information exists than is realised – what you must do is find ways of tapping this information. There are a number of possible methods:

1   Encourage internal discussion and analysis. As they go about their jobs staff and volunteers collect an enormous amount of potentially valuable information. Often they may not realise the importance of this information for your planning activity or they may feel that the organisation is not interested in hearing their information. It is particularly important that you acknowledge the value of information collected by your 'front-line' staff, those people in daily and direct contact with the users of your services.

2   Keep up-to-date information on the take-up of your services. During its pilot year Language Line kept detailed records of the number of telephone interpretations they carried out. This enabled them to demonstrate a steady increase in the demand for their services.

3   Provide users with the opportunity to comment on your organisation and its services. Charities Evaluation Services (CES) provides everyone who attends their training courses with an evaluation form as do Bromley Alcohol Advisory Services (BAAS). CES also

follow up its training courses at a later date to assess how effective organisations have been in implementing evaluation systems. This follow-up process is also used to evaluate the contribution made by CES itself. If feedback is invited, it is important to provide users with an opportunity to suggest improvements in service and that your organisation commits itself to responding to constructive criticism.

4   Review the published information that you already have. A scan of the magazines, books and publications you have in-house is likely to uncover information relevant to your analysis and will save you both time and money in investigating external sources of published information.

5   Make use of personal contacts and the networks in which you are involved. Trevor Groom, the director of BAAS, skilfully used his membership of committees to improve his understanding of the policies of key funders, for example.

Internal sources of information have a number of clear advantages. They are relatively cheap and take less time than either library visits or the organisation of surveys. Using internal sources of information is also likely to be a valuable process for your organisation. It will get more people involved in preparing the environmental analysis and will raise awareness in your organisation of the importance of collecting and analysing marketing information.

It is unlikely, however, that internal sources of information alone will be sufficient for your environmental analysis. A full assessment of all the factors likely to influence your organisation will probably require additional information from publications or users. There is also a danger that reliance on internal sources of information may result in an environmental analysis that gives too much prominence to an organisation's own view of itself. External sources should be used to add objectivity.

Once you are satisfied that you are getting the most from internal sources of information you must decide on the mix of 'secondary' and 'primary' research needed to complete your environmental analysis.

Secondary research, or desk research as it is often known, is the study of published information. Primary or field research is the activity of collecting new and specific information directly related to your own needs.

There are three main ways to carry out secondary research:

1 Study publications. This will include magazines and journals relevant to your organisation's areas of activity, publications which give useful statistics and information on social and other trends, and reviews of the implications of legislation and changes in government or funder policies.

2 Review information put out by other organisations. In addition to publications, which we have already covered, this may include press and publicity briefings and annual reports. Both of these give an indication of the plans of possible competitors. Another potential source of information is the recruitment advertising of other organisations. It is a direct indicator of plans and priorities and often contains much additional information on sources of funding, salaries and organisational structure.

3 Search libraries for information. A visit to a library can often uncover sources of information about which you were not previously aware. In addition to publications and directories, libraries increasingly offer access to computer databases that can reduce the time involved in searching for information.

Secondary market research will probably answer a lot of the questions for which you need answers. It will provide you with extensive information on the legislative, policy and funding environment you face and its general implications. Desk research will also be highly educative, revealing new sources of published information, and data on the plans of organisations similar to your own.

On the other hand desk research can be both time-consuming and frustrating. It is likely that, however many questions it does provide answers to, it will still leave you looking for information that is specific to your own organisation. In the end original primary or field research is most likely to provide you with this.

The aim of primary or field research is to develop new or original information specific to the needs of the organisation. There are several ways to do this.

1   Survey users and potential users. Using checklists or questionnaires you can directly ask your users the questions to which you need answers. Your survey can be done in person, by telephone, or by post. Alternatively you can give users who are on your premises a questionnaire to complete themselves and leave with you. A community theatre used a combination of these methods. An audience survey was used to collect information on the performances and facilities of the theatre while a survey of people at a local shopping centre gave the theatre information on its profile in the local community.

2   Set up discussion or focus groups. A focus group is a gathering of people to discuss a specific service or facility. A community centre was interested in finding out about the views of local people on its facilities. It leafleted the area and invited people to an open evening at which they offered refreshments and introduced people to the centre. A discussion was then held on how the centre could develop its services to the community.

3   Visit other organisations. You can learn a lot about how organisations similar to your own operate by visiting them and talking to key people. If a formal visit is difficult to arrange you can learn a lot about an organisation from simply sitting in its reception area. The attitudes of staff and the appearance of the organisation will give you an insight into how it treats users and the state of staff morale.

4   Attend exhibitions. Attendance at fairs or exhibitions will enable you to meet other organisations and potential users of your services. The informal discussions you will be able to have will provide you with much useful information for your business plan.

Whatever mix of primary research methods you use in preparing your environmental analysis you are likely to use a questionnaire in some form. Designing a survey questionnaire that gives you useful answers is not always easy and you should follow the four simple preparation rules below.

1   Keep the questionnaire short. If it is too long the respondent may lose interest and you will not get answers to important questions.

2   Test the questionnaire first with friends or colleagues. In this way you can check that the questions are clear and easy to understand.

3   Think carefully about the form of the questions you ask. Open-ended questions such as 'What changes in the service would you like to see?' allow the respondent to answer in their own words and can be very revealing. On the other hand closed questions such as 'Would it be helpful if the centre's opening hours were extended? Yes or No.' are easier to interpret and quantify.

4   Think carefully about the order in which you ask questions. Opening questions should try to grab the interest of the respondent. Personal questions about the respondent, eg age, sex, etc are usually put at the end of a questionnaire. Language Line, for example, did not ask whether respondents were interested in buying their service until the end of the survey and only after they had collected other information on the plans and priorities of potential users.

Primary research is most likely to give you new and exciting information about your organisation. There is also a wide range of primary research methods from which to choose and you should have no difficulty selecting an appropriate approach. On the other hand primary research can be very time-consuming, particularly if you want a large number of responses to your survey. It also requires very careful preparaton to ensure that the answers received are relevant to your information needs. The information sources and methods we have discussed are summarised in Table 6.

Table 6 Collecting Information: Sources and Methods

Internal sources	Secondary research	Primary research
Analysis and discussion	Publications	User surveys (personal, post, telephone, etc)
Information on service usage	Material from other organisations, eg annual reports, press releases, etc	Discussion or focus groups
Published information		Visits to other organisations
Contacts and networking	Library searches	
User feedback		Exhibitions

Case studies – methods of collecting information

In Table 7 the decisions of our case study organisations on research methods are summarised.

Table 7 Case Studies – Information Collection Methods

Organisation	Methods
Language Line	Review of census data to pinpoint geographical areas with highest concentration of minority language speakers
	Telephone questionnaire to local authorities, health authorities and police stations in the target areas
Interpreters' Co-op	Review of Home Office asylum statistics for the period 1984–90
	Collection of leaflets and information on potential 'competitors'
	Telephone survey of local authorities, government departments, and local solicitors practices

41

Interpreting and presenting the information

In presenting the findings of your environmental analysis you need to

- demonstrate a clear understanding of the needs and expectations of different groups of current and potential users of your organisation's services;

- identify the opportunities for, and threats to, your organisation as a result of trends and developments in its environment; and

- summarise those management actions you intend to take in order to maximise the opportunities and minimise the threats you have identified.

The first stage in this process is to summarise the findings of your information collection exercise. You should prepare a short report on the objectives of the exercise, the methods you chose, and the results in key areas. Language Line, for example, produced a summary of objectives and methods and then listed key findings under headings which included 'Awareness', 'Current Service Provision' and 'Interest in Language Line'.

The second stage is the preparation of what is known as a Strengths, Weaknesses, Opportunities and Threats (SWOT) analysis. This involves an assessment of your organisation's strengths and weaknesses in respect of services, the meeting of user needs, and sources of funding. As its title implies a SWOT analysis also involves a summary of the opportunities and threats facing the organisation. Its concepts are defined and illustrated in Table 8.

Table 8   SWOT Analysis

Strengths	What your organisation is good at; things that give your organisation an advantage, eg in getting funds *A high level of user satisfaction with its disability equality training courses (Disability Resource Team)*

Weaknesses	What your organisation is not so good at; things that put it at a disadvantage *Uncertainty among users on how best to use the service offered*
Opportunities	Events or trends that are favourable to your organisation; chances to take action *Possibility of joining with another organisation to improve services; new sources of funding*
Threats	Events or trends that are unfavourable to your organisation *A decline in statutory sources of funding*

Once you have completed your SWOT analysis you should prepare a summary of the management actions you will need to take to maximise the opportunities open to your organisation and to minimise the dangers posed by the threats you have identified. The Disability Resource Team, which at one point had the support of 10 local authorities, saw that its statutory funding could fall by as much as 50 per cent. In response it initiated a major marketing campaign to promote itself to new users and funders, and repackaged its services in response to market research findings.

The list of management actions open to you will be long. It is likely to include better marketing, improved or new services, new premises, better management, etc. At this stage you need only provide a summary of these actions. In the rest of your business plan you will produce the detail.

Summing up

Your organisation will benefit from the preparation of an environmental analysis. Such an analysis will give you an improved understanding of the opportunities open, and threats posed, to your organisation. There are three main sources of the information you need to complete an environmental analysis each with their own

43

advantages and disadvantages. Once you have collected the information you need a summary of your findings should be prepared. These findings are then interpreted in a SWOT analysis of your organisation.

Exercises

1 Decide what your organisation would most like from an environmental analysis. Make a list of the information you already have and identify the main information gaps.

2 How successful do you think you are in getting the most from internal sources of marketing information? What improvements would you like to make?

3 Draw up a research plan for your organisation indicating the mix of secondary and primary research methods you intend to use.

4 Using the preparation rules on p. 40, draw up a questionnaire to assess the views of an important group of users of your organisation's services.

5 Summarise the findings of your environmental analysis using the SWOT approach discussed.

Chapter 5
Developing a Promotional Strategy

This chapter defines marketing and explains why it is relevant to voluntary organisations, sets out guidelines for preparing a marketing strategy, details the range of marketing tools available, and outlines the steps necessary to implement a marketing strategy.

What is marketing?

We often pose this question to managers and staff attending training courses and most frequently they identify marketing as consisting of

- advertising

- public relations

- promotion

- selling

It is true that marketing involves all of these activities but advertising and promotion are in reality just the tools of marketing. Marketing is a process in which an organisation attempts to match its services to the needs of current and potential users. The marketing process has three main stages:

- the identification of the needs of users (see Chapter 4);

- adjusting the services you offer to ensure that they meet the needs you have identified; and

- providing information on these services to important groups of users.

The key to marketing is listening and responding to the needs of users and this is very well illustrated by the following example. A respite care centre offering support during the day to the relatives of people with Alzheimer's disease noticed that most statutory and voluntary centres were open only during the week. They consulted their users and found that most wanted additional support on a Saturday so that they could spend some time with other members of their family. The centre responded by offering care on Saturdays and prepared promotional material to inform both users and funders.

There is a very wide range of such marketing tools available to you and the mix of tools you choose to employ is known as the marketing mix, which is illustrated in Figure 2. This figure shows how broad an activity marketing actually is. Not only does it involve promotional activities, with which you may be more familiar, but it also includes the specification of your services, any price you charge for those services, and the means by which you provide access to your services. The key to understanding why all these activities are part of marketing is to consider the role each plays in meeting the needs of your users. You should notice that each of the main headings on Figure 2 begin with a 'P'. The marketing mix is, therefore, also known as 'the 4 Ps' – product/service, price, place and promotion. Later in this chapter we will provide several illustrations of the marketing mix chosen by different voluntary organisations.

Another way of understanding the meaning of marketing is to focus on what the person or persons responsible for marketing regard as success on the part of their organisation. To the people responsible for marketing, an organisation is successful if it is able to meet the needs of its users in the most effective way possible. Thus a service to the 'marketer' is only a good service if it actually does meet needs.

Figure 2 Scope of the Marketing Mix

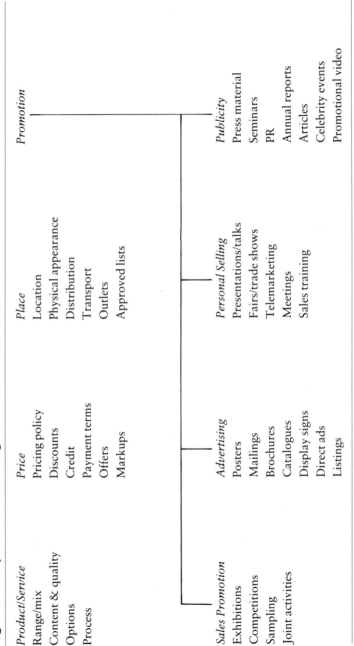

Product/Service	Price	Place	Promotion
Range/mix	Pricing policy	Location	
Content & quality	Discounts	Physical appearance	
Options	Credit	Distribution	
Process	Payment terms	Transport	
	Offers	Outlets	
	Markups	Approved lists	

Sales Promotion	Advertising	Personal Selling	Publicity
Exhibitions	Posters	Presentations/talks	Press material
Competitions	Mailings	Fairs/trade shows	Seminars
Sampling	Brochures	Telemarketing	PR
Joint activities	Catalogues	Meetings	Annual reports
	Display signs	Sales training	Articles
	Direct ads		Celebrity events
	Listings		Promotional video

The relevance of marketing to voluntary organisations

We have often found that there is suspicion among voluntary organisations of both the concept and techniques of marketing. Marketing is seen by some in the voluntary sector as inappropriate to a people-centred service or indeed as an unwanted intrusion to the delivery of services themselves. Others, however, recognise that much of what they are already doing in focusing closely on user needs and concerns is marketing activity. There are three main reasons why marketing is important to voluntary organisations:

1   A frequently mentioned strength of voluntary organisations is flexibility and responsiveness to the needs of individuals and groups of people. Marketing with its focus on matching services to needs should, therefore, be a principal ally of voluntary organisations.

2   Marketing is an important management tool for voluntary sector managers and staff. It provides numerous tools for meeting needs, for responding to opportunities and threats, and for reaching the key people (users, funders, volunteers, etc) with an interest in your organisation.

3   Marketing is also one of the best ways of maintaining contact with your organisation's environment.

In Table 9 the characteristics of an organisation which is focused on its 'markets' are contrasted to those of a product or service-focused organisation. The latter organisation is focused on its service operation and shows little interest in listening to its users. The organisation with an interest in marketing, however, focuses principally on the needs of its users and attempts to respond to the varied needs of different groups of users.

Table 9 Characteristics of Marketing and Product/Service Focused Organisations

	Type of focus	
Characteristic	*Marketing focus*	*Product/service focus*
Priority	User needs	Detail of operations
User needs	Sensitive to needs of different groups	Standard service regardless of user type
Market research	Regular/continuous	Infrequent

In conclusion, marketing will help your organisation demonstrate its commitment to users. Its techniques are, as Lovelock and Weinberg have noted in *Public and Nonprofit Marketing* (page 8), 'neutral, it can be employed . . . for both ethical and unethical ends depending on the values and goals of its user'.

Preparing a marketing strategy

There are three main steps to take in preparing a marketing strategy for your organisation:

1 Decide on your marketing objectives.

2 Group the audiences for your marketing message, a process known as segmentation.

3 Select and evaluate a mix of marketing tools that reflect your objectives and enable you to reach your target audiences.

Marketing objectives define the goals you wish your marketing strategy to achieve. These can be

● strategic objectives, eg the development of your organisation in a new direction;

● organisational objectives, eg recognition among users and funders for a high quality of service; or

- financial objectives, eg the achievement of a target level of grant or sales income.

Listing your marketing objectives will be relatively straightforward but translating them into detailed marketing activity will require that your objectives are

- *easy to prioritise*   Clarify the three or four main marketing objectives in order to select the most appropriate tools.

- *quantifiable*   Identify numbers for objectives such as new users or grant income whenever possible.

- *realistic*   Marketing requires patience and a willingness to wait for results. Over ambitious objectives will put your organisation under great strain and result in disappointment.

- *consistent*   Try to minimise the potential for conflict between your marketing objectives, eg between financial objectives such as profit on trading activities and organisational objectives such as a reputation as a caring organisation.

Case study – marketing objectives

Charities Evaluation Services
Charities Evaluation Services (CES) was established in 1990 to promote good evaluation practice throughout the voluntary sector. Its principal services include advice and training in self-evaluation and the provision of an external evaluation service for funders and voluntary organisations. By early 1993 it had a central office staff of five and regional offices in Northern Ireland, Wales and London and Southern England.

Initially CES was funded by grants from a diverse group of funders that included the Home Office, several charitable trusts and corporate donors. While some of these grants were renewed beyond their original terms, others were not, and CES's management realised that it had to raise its profile through marketing. Until 1993 CES had restricted its marketing activity while it set up the structures to respond to demand. Its business plan for 1993/4, therefore, required a fresh statement of marketing objectives. CES decided on six main marketing objectives:

strategic objectives

- to establish market leadership in the provision of training courses in self-evaluation for voluntary organisations

- to secure a growing stream of enquiries for training and external evaluation

- to promote publications on good practice to funders and voluntary organisations

organisational objectives

- to raise the profile of CES and establish it as the leading evaluation agency in the UK

- to establish and fill a definite number of training courses for voluntary organisations across each of CES's regions of operation

financial objectives

- to ensure that CES generates sufficient income from grants and revenue generating assignments to sustain and develop the organisation

---

Once the marketing objectives are set you need to decide which groups make up the target audience for your marketing activity. This process is known as segmentation and is based on the fact that different groups of users of a service are likely to have different needs and perceptions of the service offered. Segmentation, therefore, involves the grouping of users according to shared characteristics such as age, ethnic identity or type of organisation. The identified groups are then known as market segments.

The importance of segmentation to a business plan can be

illustrated by the difficulties alcohol counselling agencies have experienced in reaching problem drinkers from ethnic minorities. While evidence suggests that alcohol misuse is as significant here as elsewhere, most agencies have found that people from minority groups are under-represented among their clients. A general as opposed to targeted service appeared to be failing to meet the needs of this group. As a result agencies have tried many ways to improve the match between services and client needs. These have included the appointment of counsellors from minority groups, outreach work and the design of targeted promotional material.

Case study – segmentation

Occupational therapy project

A district health authority was planning to extend its occupational therapy programme by supporting a screen printing workshop staffed by people recovering from psychiatric problems. The feasibility of the project depended on its ability to earn money, in addition to the health authority grant, from the sale of printed goods. In order to decide the service mix and marketing strategy of the project the managers needed to know who the potential customers of the workshop might be.

To identify customers the project's management interviewed local organisations and visited projects with similar aims. On the basis of this research the managers were able to identify three 'market segments' to which marketing activity would have to be directed:

- individuals living within a one-mile radius of the workshop

- institutions such as local schools, voluntary organisations and community groups

- commercial buyers such as bookstores, local companies and museums with shops and catalogues

The success of the approaches to reaching minority ethnic groups has yet to be conclusively established. What is important, however, is the recognition that different groups of users have different needs and that this may well require a specific service response. Your business plan should show that you have considered these issues and their implications for your marketing activity. You should, therefore, identify the target groups or segments for your marketing strategy, and prepare a general statement of how you intend to meet the needs of each target group. Such a statement is sometimes known as a position statement and some examples are given in Table 10. A position statement will help you choose the marketing tools most suited to your organisation.

Table 10   Examples of Position Statements

Agency/service	Position statement
Occupational therapy project	A rehabilitation initiative that offers current and potential supporters in the local community an attractive and quality range of products
Publication	A comprehensive and focused information service that is contemporary, attractively priced, and enables subscribers to save time in finding information
Respite care	To provide relief from the burden of care at times that fit in with the family needs of carers

As we saw in Figure 2, you can choose from a wide range of marketing tools in putting together your marketing strategy. In practice your choice will be influenced by four factors:

- the knowledge available on how important audiences learn about the services provided by your organisation;

- the marketing objectives you have set;

- the information available about the needs of different user groups and decisions on how you intend to respond (segmentation and position statement);

- the total resources available. It is unlikely that you would have the time and the money to do all the marketing you desire.

In selecting a marketing mix for your organisation you should also distinguish between tools that are intended for the organisation as a whole and those that will be used to market individual products or services.

Some examples of the marketing mix adopted by voluntary organisations are set out in Table 11 which shows both the diverse range of marketing activity of a small selection of voluntary organisations and the importance of adapting products and services to meet user needs. It also shows how innovative the organisations were. The occupational therapy project, for example, contacted local schools to organise a competition to design a card for the launch of the project itself. Creative marketing is clearly not just a tool of expensive advertising agencies.

Table 11   Illustration of the Marketing Mix

Organisation	*Marketing Mix Selected*
Charities	Publicity – articles, seminars, newsletter
Evaluation Services	Advertising – direct advertising in journals, leaflets
	Personal selling – networking and liaison
	Service mix – introduction of open training courses
Occupational	Products – screen printed greeting cards,
therapy project	Price – between 1.5 and 2 times cost
	Publicity – articles, celebrity events
	Promotion – design events and competitions
Disability	Service mix – introduction of new service

Resource Team	packages, review of mix Promotion – targeted mailing of personnel and training functions Personal selling – conferences, presentations
Interpreters' Co-operative	Promotion – letter and leaflet to possible clients Publicity – press releases Sales promotion – offer of free trial usage Price – preparation of a rate card

Implementing the marketing strategy

The implementation of your marketing strategy will comprise four main activities:

- the setting of a budget for marketing

- the allocation of responsibility for implementation

- the specification of systems to collect and manage marketing information

- the identification of constraints on the implementation of the strategy

Because it is unlikely that an organisation has the time and the resources to undertake all the marketing activity it would like, it is imperative that the cost of each marketing proposal and its relative priority be identified.

Marketing activity can be costed from records of previous marketing, quotes from printers of leaflets and other material, and published rates for advertising in journals and magazines. Much costing can be done using readily available information. For example, to send out 300 leaflets by first class post will cost at least £72 – the price of 300 stamps at 24p each. You may also want to include the costs of other materials, such as the leaflets and envelopes used in the mailing, in the estimate.

Priorities should be determined by the marketing objectives. For example, if getting a higher profile among potential users is a priority, then measures to secure publicity such as mailing leaflets and public relations are likely to be important. If, however, a reputation for service quality is the most important marketing objective, then a focus on the nature and content of your service mix will be the most appropriate. A helpful way of reconciling marketing priorities with limited finances is to split your proposals into essential items and desirable items. The essential items will be introduced first with the desirable items pursued at a later date if more resources become available. An example of how to present a budget for marketing is given in Table 12.

Table 12   A Budget for Marketing

Budget heading	Plans and expenditure	
Essential items		
Leaflets	New leaflet on services	£3,000
Market research	Regular user surveys	£350
Mailing campaign	Postage; freelance support	£800
Sub-total		£4,150
Desirable items		
Advertising	Adverts in relevant journals	£600
Video	Video on the organisation	£1,000
Sub-total		£1,600
Total costs		£5,750

The marketing section of the business plan will lack credibility if you do not specify who will have responsibility for co-ordinating the implementation of your marketing strategy, be it one person or a team. A team approach will increase the skills and resources available for marketing and can help build confidence if you are new to marketing. On the other hand, the efforts of a team may be more difficult to co-ordinate and delays may result.

Whether you nominate an individual or a team, their responsibilities should include:

- co-ordinating specific activity such as the preparation of marketing material and the organisation of mailings

- communicating the strategy to other people in the organisation

- monitoring and evaluating the impact of marketing activity

- organising any staff training in marketing that may be needed

Since marketing is an activity which affects every aspect of an organisation's service there can be no general rule about who in the organisation should have final responsibility for it. All we can say is that the person or persons responsible for marketing should have sufficient authority to ensure that co-ordination takes place and the ability to liaise with people across the whole organisation.

In order to review the effectiveness of your marketing activity and to keep up-to-date with opportunities and threats you should maintain a system for collecting marketing information which should include:

- internal records such as mailing and contact lists, details of responses to specific marketing activity, user feedback and details of contacts with funders;

- marketing intelligence in the form of publications and subscriptions to relevant magazines, information on the activities of 'competitors', and information on social trends and funding policies; and

- regular market research.

As we argued in Chapter 4, you should encourage all members of staff and volunteers to become involved in the collection of marketing information. Their direct contact with the users of your services makes them an invaluable marketing asset.

It is probable that the implementation of your marketing strategy will take place in phases in order to reflect:

- priorities in respect of target user segments

- resource constraints

- the need for effective planning and review of the strategy

Your business plan should, therefore, include a timetable for the implementation of your marketing strategy. This should specify target dates for the completion of different activities and identify mechanisms for assessing both the progress and success of marketing initiatives.

Case study – Implementation of a marketing strategy

Disability Resource Team

The Disability Resource Team (DRT) set up a team to co-ordinate its marketing strategy. The team met once a week, was chaired by the deputy director and included staff from DRT's publications and information sections as well as a consultant who had helped develop the strategy. The team had clear priorities:

- personnel and training officers were identified as the principal targets for marketing material

- the country was divided into a number of sectors

- contact names for a sector were identified and written to and a procedure for following up letters was agreed

- the results for each sector were reviewed before a new sector was approached

Each meeting of the team reviewed progress with the implementation of the strategy and discussed how the strategy might be amended and supported by other activity. In this way a programme of public relations and press activity was identified and successfully implemented. The confidence of the team grew with each successive meeting. 'Although the team took time to develop a sense of purpose we were gradually able to shift the focus of the organisation towards the clients we needed in order to survive', concluded the deputy director.

Summing up

Marketing is the process of matching your organisation's services to the needs of current and potential users. The preparation of a marketing strategy for inclusion in your business plan involves three main steps. You will need to set marketing objectives, identify the target groups for your marketing message, and select a range of marketing methods to reach your targets. Your marketing strategy will be completed by the preparation of a budget for marketing and the identification of how you intend to implement the strategy.

Exercises

1 Review the scope of the marketing mix on p. 46 and prepare a summary of your organisation's current marketing activity.

2 What benefits do you think your organisation could realise from more extensive marketing?

3 What are your organisation's principal 'market segments'? In what ways do these segments differ from each other?

4 Draw up a plan for implementing your marketing strategy. Will you use a team or an individual to co-ordinate implementation? What are the reasons for your choice?

Chapter 6
Working Effectively

This chapter sets out the key requirements of effective working, and discusses management information systems and other operational issues of importance to the business plan. It also explains the importance of monitoring and evaluation and the importance of systems for quality assurance.

In Chapters 4 and 5 we considered how to investigate your organisation's environment and develop a marketing strategy which reflected the needs and concerns of your clients. In this and the two following chapters our focus will be on the structures and systems you will need to support your business plan.

The role of people and equipment

The effectiveness of your organisation will to a large degree depend on the quality of the people and equipment you employ. The business plan should, therefore, describe the role of both people and equipment in the delivery of services.

In respect of the input of people your business plan should describe the following:

- the activities of the people you will be working with, eg direct service provision, administration, fund raising, management, etc;

- the skills and qualifications of the people involved in each of the activities you have identified;

- the respective roles of paid staff, volunteers and, where appropriate, of management committee members, in delivering the service you offer; and

- the total amount (hours, days, etc) of people resources you will have available for the different activities of your organisation. This will give you an indication of the capacity of your organisation.

Planning for staff requirements is discussed in greater detail in Chapter 7. Here we spend some more time on the issue of capacity. Staff capacity is basically the maximum amount of staff time in either hours, days or weeks that is available for work. It is important for planning purposes that you have a reliable estimate of what this capacity is. For example, if you have set a target of providing a certain number of advice or counselling sessions you need to know how many hours of adviser time is necessary to provide these sessions. A framework for working out your staff capacity is described below and illustrated in the case of Language Line.

A starting point for estimating your staff capacity is to calculate the number of hours a full-time member of staff has available in a year. If they work a 35-hour week it is tempting to assume that their capacity is 52 (weeks) multiplied by 35 (hours) or 1,820 hours a year. This figure makes no allowance, however, for holidays or sick leave. A sensible assumption would be that each member of staff has a total of seven weeks' holiday and sick leave. The new estimate of staff capacity is 45 (weeks) multiplied by 35 (hours) or 1,575 hours a year.

Now if this person is involved in direct service delivery such as the provision of advice it is unlikely that they will be able to provide advice for every 'available' hour. They will also need to complete paperwork or consult other sources of information to ensure that their advice is accurate. This will reduce their availability for service provision. If we assume that the staff member spends one-third of their time on various administrative duties, then only 30 weeks of the year will be spent on service delivery. The number of hours available for service provision will now be 30 (weeks) multiplied by 35 (hours) or 1,050 hours a year.

What is clear from this analysis is that, when very reasonable assumptions about true availability are made, the initial estimate of staff capacity is very quickly reduced. It is vital, therefore, that you make realistic assumptions about capacity and indicate in your business plan how you are going to provide sufficient resources to achieve your service targets. The role of volunteers can be very important in this context. Your plan should, therefore, describe how volunteers will contribute to the delivery of services and provide information on how the input of volunteers will be co-ordinated.

Case study – capacity management

Language Line
Before entering negotiations for service contracts Language Line wanted to be sure that it had sufficient capacity to meet the likely demand for telephone interpreting. In estimating staff capacity the project made the following assumptions:

- it was possible for an interpreter to complete 6 telephone interpreting sessions an hour

- each interpreter worked a 35-hour week and was available for 45 weeks a year – the annual availability of each interpreter was, therefore, 1,575 hours

The apparent capacity of each interpreter was, then, estimated by multiplying annual availability in hours (1,575) by the number of calls possible in each hour (6). This gave an estimated capacity of 9,450 calls per interpreter.

After some consideration, however, the director decided that this estimate was too high. Firstly, the work of the interpreters needed to be varied. It was not reasonable to expect them to be tied to the phone for seven hours a day. Secondly, the estimate of six interpreting sessions per hour assumed that one call would be directly followed by another. It was more likely that there would be gaps between calls or that a request for a telephone interpretation would be made when an interpreter was already busy.

The estimate of capacity was reduced to take account of these factors. It was assumed that interpreters would spend 40% of their time on other duties reducing their hours of availability to 945 a year. Secondly, the director assumed that extra capacity would be needed to ensure that all requests for service could be dealt with. It was estimated that this would reduce the availability of an individual interpreter by a further quarter to 708.75 hours a year. In terms of calls the capacity of each interpreter was now estimated at 4,252 a year, less than half the original estimate.

It is equally important that your business plan details the role that equipment will play in service delivery. You should provide information on two types of equipment:

- office technology such as computers and software

- larger items of capital equipment such as transport and facilities to improve access to your services

You should provide a list of the main items of equipment that you have or would like to acquire, and should list the principal benefits of this equipment to your organisation and its users. In respect of capital equipment these benefits are likely to include improved quality of service and the realisation of your commitment to provide equal access to services for all groups of users. The benefits to your organisation of office automation will include:

- improved productivity, eg in administration, responding to enquiries, etc;

- improved professionalism (For example, the continuing fall in the price of items such as laser printers is improving the access of voluntary organisations to equipment that improves the quality of document presentation.);

- assistance in monitoring and evaluating the activity of your organisation (Computer databases, for instance, may help in the storage and analysis of service records.); and

- the development of staff skills and confidence.

When you are considering a change in your use of equipment, such as increased office automation or the introduction of systems such as desk top publishing, you should undertake a cost–benefit analysis of the change. Desk top publishing is one example where organisations tend to focus exclusively on benefits and neglect the costs. The benefits of improved presentation and lower production costs are well known but the hidden costs of expensive and lengthy staff training are often not provided for.

Management information systems

Accurate and reliable systems of management information are important for several reasons:

1 They help managers to take decisions and exercise control over important activities.

2 They provide information on the way in which the resources of the organisation are being used.

3 They assist funders and management committees in maintaining accountability and monitoring value for money.

Your business plan should detail how you intend to develop and maintain appropriate systems of management information. In addition to marketing information systems, which we discussed in Chapter 5, you will need to maintain systems that cover:

- *the activity of staff and volunteers* Like many voluntary organisations you are likely to have less staff than you might wish. With staff time so valuable it is important to ensure that it is used to greatest effect. A good way of monitoring the use of staff time is to ask staff and regular volunteers to keep activity records or time sheets. These will record the amount of time spent each week or month on different activities. Such records will help you assess whether your organisation's priorities are being accurately reflected in actual activity and to identify areas where more resources would help.

The completion and analysis of activity records can often be time-consuming, especially if your organisation is small. If you find this to be the case then you should follow the practice of many organisations who collect activity records for one week in each month or for one month in each six-month period.

- *personnel issues* We will discuss personnel systems in more detail in Chapter 7. It is likely that your management information systems will cover staff performance and appraisal, sickness and holiday records and details of staff turnover.

- *enquiries made to your organisation* For many organisations information on enquiries received is very important. It indicates the demand for the services you provide and provides information on the success of your organisation in reaching target groups of users. Your business plan should state how you intend to record and monitor enquiries, and how you plan to use the information this will give you. At the Disability Resource Team, for example, a standard enquiries form was developed. Duplicate copies were held at each desk and every member of staff was briefed on how to complete the form. Once completed a copy was sent to DRT's information officer for recording and monitoring while the duplicate was sent to a member of staff who could answer the enquiry.

- *finance* We will be discussing financial management systems in Chapter 8. Such systems will have two main functions:

  – the monitoring and control of income and expenditure

  – the budgeting and costing of your services

In designing the management information systems for your organisation you should:

1 Ensure that they are appropriate to your needs. Avoid making the systems too complex and time-consuming to manage, or the costs of keeping the systems will be greater than the value of the information you receive.

2 Consider the needs of those people, eg funders, management committee members, etc, to whom you have to report information. You will save time both in explaining your reports and revising your systems if you listen to the opinions of those who receive information from them.

3 Consider informal as well as formal methods of generating management information. If your organisation is relatively small, for example, meetings and informal discussion are likely to be an important source of management information. Management forums are also a good means of communicating management information.

4 Consider ways in which you can use computer technology to save time in the collection and analysis of management information. For example, you can set up reporting forms on a computer, and directly enter and print the information when you need to.

Monitoring and evaluation

One of the main roles of your management information systems will be to help you monitor and evaluate your services. Since monitoring and evaluation are increasingly seen as important by funders and voluntary organisations alike it is worth pausing to consider what is meant by these terms. According to the Charities Evaluation Services monitoring is the collection and analysis of 'factual' information, while evaluation is assessing the value of an activity involving the measurement of performance and learning from experience.

There are many reasons why your business plan should detail how you intend to monitor and evaluate your activities. Essentially monitoring and evaluation is important to you:

- as a means of assessing the results of your organisation's activities;

- as a means of identifying improvements to the services you offer; and

- as a means of helping you control and plan your activities.

It is also important to your organisation's funders and supporters:

- as a means of ensuring accountability for money spent on, or donated to, your organisation;

- as a means of ensuring value for money; and

- as an influence on the development of future funding policies.

Monitoring and evaluation should, therefore, have a prominent place in your business plan. The monitoring and evaluation checklist below suggests what should be in the business plan as well as some examples of what might be included on each item.

Monitoring and evaluation checklist

What you intend to monitor and evaluate

Number of contacts; number of users; categories of user (eg sex, ethnic origin, etc); how users learnt about the service; user views on the service; service outcomes

How you intend to monitor and evaluate

Review meetings; collection of information through forms; measurement of service against standards or performance indicators

How you will report on your findings

Regular internal management reports; quarterly reports to funders; publication of statistics and annual reviews

Responsibility for collection, analysis and taking action

Specific individuals; management team; management committee/ trustees; director

How the information will be used to improve quality of service

Discussion forums; modification of the service (eg extended hours); improvement to service features (eg improved service environment)

The final item on the checklist provides the link to our next subject. Although the collection and analysis of monitoring information is both useful and interesting you will only maximise the value of the information by actually using it to improve the quality of what you offer your clients.

Quality assurance

There is an extensive literature on service quality, much of it aiming to define quality, and some of this is referred to in Appendix 4. Our concern is with how you should include material on quality in your business plan and for this purpose a simple definition of quality will be adequate. We shall define service quality as effectiveness in achieving the objectives of an organisation, and will look at two ways in which your business plan can address the issue of quality.

The first of the two methods is to detail how the process, outputs, and outcomes of your activities will ensure quality of service. They are defined as follows:

- *Process*   the methods used to provide a service; includes the policies and procedures of the organisation

- *Outputs*   measures of the amount of service delivered

- *Outcomes*   the consequences or results of the service activity

Table 13 illustrates how this approach was applied by an alcohol counselling agency. You should try to identify similar standards and

Table 13   Quality Measures – Alcohol Counselling Agency

Process	Outputs	Outcomes
External standards	Number of enquiries	Evidence of changed
Staff recruitment and training	Number of counselling sessions	drinking behaviour
Monitoring and evaluation	Value for money measures	Client feedback
Operational policies and procedures	• Sessions per counsellor	Achievement of agreed care goals
Manual on referrals and client assessment	• Unit cost per session	Planned exit from care as % of client exits
	• % of counselling hours taken up	Continued referrals from key agencies
	Percentage of contacts attending sessions	

performance indicators in each of the three categories that are relevant to your organisation. Your business plan should summarise these measures and provide some explanation of why they are important to your organisation's areas of activity.

We have often heard it argued that while it is relatively easy to identify measures for the process and output of service, it is very difficult to develop measures of service outcome for voluntary organisations. This reflects the difficulty of quantifying outcomes for services that are focused on caring for individual people. While this is true, we believe that it is possible to identify appropriate measures of service outcome. The alcohol counselling agency, for example, chose to distinguish between 'hard' or quantifiable measures of outcome, such as reduced drinking, and 'soft' measures such as achievement of the goals the individual agreed when starting counselling.

As an alternative to the process, outputs, outcomes approach you could consider including a quality plan in your business plan. A quality plan summarises your organisation's commitment to quality and lists the systems you will adopt to ensure service quality. It should include:

- the principles or values of quality which your organisation holds, eg belief in equal opportunities and the involvement of service users;

- a summary of how you intend to collect and analyse information on service performance;

- details of how you plan to develop your 'human resources' (staff, volunteers, etc) in order to improve service quality; and

- a summary of how you will collect information on the opinions of users of your services, and how you will respond to these opinions (eg dealing with complaints, improving service, etc.)

You will have noticed that there are some similarities between the two approaches. You should choose the approach which most fits your organisation and which you feel most confident in using.

There is growing discussion of the relevance to voluntary organisations of formal certificates of quality. The best known of these is BS5750, the standard produced by the British Standards Institution (BSI). The advantages and disadvantages of an application for BS5750 are discussed by Alan Lawrie in *Quality of Service – Measuring Performance for Voluntary Organisations* which is published jointly by NCVO and the Directory of Social Change. If you decide that an application would be right for your organisation, then your business plan should describe why and how you intend to apply. In particular you should detail who will be responsible for the application and identify the time and cost that will be involved.

Other operational issues

There are other operational issues which you should consider at this stage of the business planning process:

- *legal issues* You should review whether any of the objectives and activities you are proposing have any legal implications for your organisation. For example, will you need to establish a trading company or change the legal status of your organisation? If any legal changes are necessary your business plan should provide details, explaining why the changes are necessary and how they will be implemented. A timetable for making the legal arrangements should be provided and you should indicate who will provide you with any legal advice that may be required.

- *suitability of premises*   At this stage of the process you should review whether your organisation's premises enable you to deliver an effective service. If your conclusion is that the premises are unsuitable then your plan should include a specification for new premises. At Language Line, for example, the business plan concluded that additional space was required for the project's management, for interpreters to complete administrative tasks, and for holding meetings and presentations on the project. You should also describe your plans for finding new space and provide an estimate of the additional cost to your organisation of the new facilities.

Summing up

All voluntary organisations need systems to help them work effectively and your business plan should detail how you will establish and maintain the necessary systems. The plan should detail the role of both people and equipment in delivering your organisation's services. In addition the plan should provide details of the management information systems you will use and indicate how you plan to monitor and evaluate the quality of your services.

Exercises

1   Using the techniques described estimate your staff capacity in hours per year. Will this give you sufficient staff resources to fulfil your service plans? If not, how will you attempt to increase capacity?

2   Review your current systems for providing management informa-

tion. What are the strengths and weaknesses of these systems? How do you plan to develop the systems your organisation needs?

3 Referring to the monitoring and evaluation checklist on pp. 67–8 summarise how you intend to monitor and evaluate your services.

4 What indicators of service quality do you plan to use? What measures of service outcome can you specify for your organisation?

Chapter 7
Staffing and Management

This chapter describes the task of planning staff requirements and the importance of clearly identifying how to allocate and co-ordinate key tasks. It also specifies what the plan should say about the organisation's management structures and emphasises the importance of specifying systems for staff motivation and involvement.

Having the right people and management arrangements is vital to making your business plan a reality. For this reason the section on staffing and management will, after the finance section, be the most closely read section of your plan.

Planning your staff requirements

To plan for your staff requirements you should begin by estimating:

- *the numbers of staff you will need over the period of the plan*
  This will be closely related to your service objectives and to your assessment of the staff capacity you will need (see Chapter 6).

- *the mix of skills you will need from your staff*   You should list the skills that you believe are essential to achieving your objectives together with the qualifications and experience that you will require your staff to have. For example, if you are running a community nursery you may require all nursery staff to have an NNEB qualification or you may accept that, for some staff, experience plus a commitment to attend training is sufficient. What is important is that you are clear about both the skills you need and how you will assess whether your staff have the necessary skills.

The next step is to specify how you will acquire or develop the staff skills you require. You will have three main options:

1 *training and development of your existing staff* Your plan should detail the training needs of your staff and state how you intend to provide the necessary training. The Disability Resource Team (DRT), for example, identified training in marketing and financial management as priorities and invited a trainer to provide courses that were customised to its needs. In addition to its main priorities, DRT also identified a number of areas, such as customer care and the use of computers, for further staff training. Your plan should also identify a budget for training and clarify how the budget will be allocated.

2 *recruitment of new staff* It is likely that development of existing staff will need to be supplemented by the employment of new staff. Your plan should state how many people will need to be recruited and for what roles. In addition you should provide information on how you intend to recruit the necessary staff, eg open advertisement, head-hunting, etc and on any employment policies, such as equal opportunities procedure, that you intend to follow. Finally, since recruitment advertising can be expensive, you should stipulate a recruitment budget.

3 *the recruitment and development of volunteers* Volunteers, as we saw in Chapter 6, can help your organisation increase its capacity for service delivery. They are also a way of involving a wide range of people in your organisation and of tapping useful skills and experience. Many voluntary organisations draw up a list of the skills they would like to find through their volunteers and use a variety of means including networking and advertising to find people. Your business plan should detail the contribution you

want from volunteers and state how you intend to develop a skilled force of volunteers.

Allocating and co-ordinating tasks

Most funders will agree that, after financial crises, the biggest source of problems for voluntary organisations is the failure

- to allocate different tasks such as finance, marketing or service delivery to different members of staff, and

- to develop ways of co-ordinating the tasks that have been allocated in order to ensure that the organisation achieves its objectives.

The consequences of failing to be clear about the allocation and co-ordination of tasks are serious. Important tasks will not be completed and services will not be delivered. Staff morale will fall and both users and funders will become dissatisfied with the organisation. Ultimately the organisation may collapse. It is essential, therefore, that your business plan provides a clear statement of how you will allocate tasks and demonstrates how co-ordination of tasks will be accomplished.

Start by listing key organisational tasks such as finance, personnel, etc. Then list who will be responsible for each task and to whom the person responsible for each task will report. An example of this approach is illustrated in Table 14. It shows that responsibility for tasks can be shared between staff, management committee members, and volunteers.

It is important to specify who each person reports to in order to provide accountability for the way tasks are performed and to create a framework for co-ordinating your organisation's activities. There are essentially three ways in which you can co-ordinate tasks:

- by informal means such as discussions between individuals

- by means of teams which meet regularly to discuss progress with agreed plans

- by means of a formal structure of line management which gives authority for co-ordination to specific individuals

Each has its advantages and disadvantages.

Table 14   Allocating Tasks

Task	Responsibility	Reporting to
Preparing the work programme	Director	Management committee
Setting goals	Management committee	Funders
Marketing	Director	Management committee
Personnel systems	Personnel officer	Director
Administration	Admin officer	Director
Training services	Training officer	Director
Reception and secretarial	Secretary and volunteers	Admin officer

Informal mechanisms are well suited to small voluntary organisations where people are in constant contact with each other and are, therefore, able to inform each other about management needs on a regular basis. Such mechanisms also appeal to the democratic culture of many voluntary organisations. The danger with informal co-ordination, however, is that responsibility for key tasks can become blurred when no one person has ultimate responsibility for ensuring that plans are adhered to. Individual members of staff will often pursue activities of interest to themselves which are not priorities for the organisation as a whole. Some of the problems of informal mechanisms of co-ordination are illustrated in the case study on 'Allocating and co-ordinating tasks'.

A team approach to co-ordination recognises some of the difficulties of informal mechanisms and provides a structure for regularly reviewing the performance of tasks. The challenge is to develop a common sense of identity and team purpose. To succeed the team will need to agree objectives, to have structured agenda, and to nominate someone to chair the meetings.

Both informal and team methods of co-ordination will have limitations if your organisation grows in size. With larger size will come more formal mechanisms of co-ordination and the introduction of structures of line management. A typical line management structure will involve a director who reports to the management committee and supervises staff who are responsible for different activities. These staff may themselves be responsible for managing other less senior staff. Despite the fact that formal systems of co-ordination are less democratic than the other mechanisms, they are widespread in the voluntary sector.

Case study – allocating and co-ordinating tasks

Community Video Project

The Community Video Project (CVP) was established in 1985 to provide community access to video editing and production facilities. By 1989 it employed four staff and was involved in video training and production. It had secured funding from a diverse range of sources including the local authority and the regional arts board. As the project grew it became increasingly aware of problems with its management and administrative arrangements. Moreover the policies of its funders were changing – to win funding in this environment CVP knew that it must find solutions to its problems.

Prior to writing its business plan CVP decided to conduct an organisational review. The conclusions of the review made uncomfortable reading. Essentially the review concluded that the management committee, which comprised experts on video production, were unwilling to take responsibility for management. The ideology of the project was non-hierarchical with each member of staff enjoying equal pay and status. The consequence was that the decisions reached at staff meetings were often not implemented and no one could say who was responsible for implementation. It was also unclear who was responsible for important tasks such as goal-setting and administration. Job descriptions were vague and such systems as existed were routinely ignored. The review concluded that unless a new organisational structure could be agreed the project would be 'overwhelmed by changes in its environment'.

In response to the review CVP developed proposals for its business plan. These recognised that someone had to take responsibility for general management and for ensuring that administrative systems were established and kept to. The plan also concluded that responsibility for training, video services and administration should be given respectively to three different members of staff. A mechanism for securing the closer involvement of the management committee was also required.

In 1990 CVP appointed a general manager to co-ordinate activity and a staff liaison sub-committee of the management committee was established. This new committee was to meet with the general manager between management committee meetings to monitor the implementation of CVP's work programme and to support the efforts of staff. The job descriptions of the other staff were rewritten to reflect their new responsibilities. Although the future remained difficult, CVP at last felt confident that they could confront the challenges that lay ahead.

One implication of the case study on 'Allocating and Co-ordinating Tasks' is that clear job descriptions will help you allocate and co-ordinate tasks. You should be willing to review job descriptions on a regular basis to ensure that they are clear about the division of responsibilities and reflect the changing needs of your organisation.

Management structures

Once you have specified how tasks are to be allocated and co-ordinated you should provide a summary of the management structure of your organisation. An organisation chart will help the

Figure 3   Organisation Chart

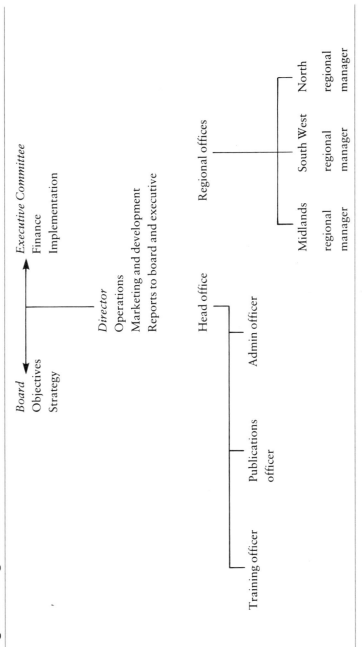

readers of your plan to understand how your organisation is structured and to picture how responsibilities are divided between staff, management committee and volunteers. Your organisation chart should include details of

- management or executive committees to whom staff report
- the identity and responsibilities of senior management
- staff positions and responsibilities

An example of an organisation chart is given in Figure 3. In addition to showing how responsibilities are divided the chart also gives the reader an indication of the number of staff or activities for which individual members of staff are responsible. An assessment can then be made of whether your organisation has sufficient management resources to achieve its objectives. For example, in Figure 3 the director has responsibility for managing six staff (three of whom are in separate offices), for operations and marketing, and for reporting to the management and executive committee of the organisation. There is an obvious danger that the director may become overstretched and, as a result, that the management of the organisation may suffer. The organisation should consider supporting the director with an assistant or deputy.

At this stage of the business planning process you should describe how you intend to tap the skills and expertise of your management committee. Your business plan should describe the contribution that you hope the committee will make and identify the mechanisms that will channel the energies of the committee. For instance, you may want to establish sub-committees of the management committee on areas, such as fund raising or personnel, in which committee members have experience. Alternatively you might identify individual commit-tee members who can give direct help to members of staff in performing their jobs.

There is a growing recognition that, like staff and volunteers, trustees and members of management committees need support and training to do their job effectively. Your business plan should, therefore, indicate how you will induct, support and train management committee members.

Motivating staff

Many thousands of people work for voluntary organisations out of a commitment to their values and culture. It is important, however, that this commitment is not taken for granted. The motivation of your staff is important for several reasons:

1 Unhappy or demoralised staff are unlikely to deliver the quality services which are necessary to secure continued funding.

2 Voluntary organisations focus on the needs of individual people. Valuing your staff is central to this approach.

3 Frequent departures of staff can be very costly in terms of recruiting replacements and will disrupt services.

4 A stable and dedicated staff team will enhance your organisation's reputation with users and funders alike.

Your business plan should, therefore, detail how you will motivate your staff. In particular you should specify:

1 *how staff will be rewarded both in terms of salary and other benefits* It is important that your reward structure is clear to staff and that your contracts of employment specify their terms of employment (hours of work, salary, etc) and provides detail of other benefits. If, for example, your organisation wishes to provide maternity leave or pay in addition to that offered by the state, then the contracts of employment issued by your organisation should detail how employees qualify for additional rights.

2 *the systems that will be used to appraise staff performance* You should provide information on the nature and frequency of performance reviews. If new members of staff have a period of probation before they become permanent employees, then your plan should give details and indicate how the review will work. It is

vital that you detail the criteria that will be used to assess performance and state who will conduct reviews.

It is also essential that your performance review system is open, consistent and fair. In one advice agency, for example, the director used different criteria to judge each advice worker and made individual arrangements with staff over holidays and hours of work. Not surprisingly a feeling of mistrust developed among the staff group and service quality deteriorated.

3 *the details of induction and other training that will be received by all members of staff* Many organisations neglect induction training and the opportunity it gives to build staff commitment and establish new working relationships. You should have a clear programme of induction training and attempt to give new staff members an understanding of all the activities of your organisation.

4 *the details of systems for involving staff in the management of the organisation* These will be particularly important if you have a hierarchical or line management structure and your business plan should describe how staff will be consulted about major plans.

You may also want to make reference in your plan to any other personnel systems operated by your organisation. These could include disciplinary and grievance procedures, and, if appropriate to your services, specific arrangements for health and safety.

Case study – performance appraisal

Charities Evaluation Services
CES has a strong commitment, for reasons of both staff development and service quality, to a system of staff appraisal. Altogether it lists 11 objectives for its system of performance appraisal. These include the identification of each employee's strengths and weaknesses, the recognition and encouragement of good work and the identification of training needs.

The review itself, which is undertaken by the director of CES, covers the following:

- a review of the job description in the light of the development of workload

- employee strengths and weaknesses

- employee motivation

- performance in respect of progress against targets, the use of initiative, accuracy, etc

- co-operation and communication with other members of staff and outside organisations

- training and development needs

On the basis of the review the director and member of staff identify an action plan aimed at strengthening performance over the next 12 months. The director herself is appraised, using the same procedure, by a member of the management committee.

This system has worked well and CES are seeking to develop it in order to provide even closer focus on the key tasks that require effective performance.

Other issues

There are other issues under the heading of staffing and management that you should include at this stage of the business planning process:

1 *CVs of key staff* The viability of your organisation depends to a large extent on the skills and experience of key staff, and funders do like to know if your organisation has access to the people who will make their investment worthwhile. You should, therefore, prepare brief biographies of key staff that will give the readers of your plan a feeling for their backgrounds and abilities. Inclusion of such biographies will also give your plan a personal touch, adding interest for its readers.

2 *employment and the law* The recruitment and employment of people has many legal implications for your organisation. Appendix 4 lists some useful sources of information in this area and you should show in your business plan that you take your responsibilities as an employer seriously.

3 *staff turnover* However strongly motivated your staff, it is likely that, for a variety of reasons, some will leave your organisation. Staff turnover provides a measure of the scale of such departures. If, for example, you have 10 employees and 3 of these leave during the year, then you will have a staff turnover rate of 30 per cent. High staff turnover rates can disrupt services and create a bad impression with funders. As we noted above, high staff turnover is also costly. If, for example, it costs an average of £2,000 to recruit a new member of staff, then a 30 per cent turnover rate for an organisation with 10 employees will result in the recruitment of 3 new staff and costs of £6,000 a year. If it could reduce staff turnover to 10 per cent, then it would save £4,000 in recruitment costs.

Your business plan should, therefore, include a target for staff turnover and describe how you will monitor people's reasons for leaving your organisation. If you interview each member of staff who wishes to leave your organisation about their reasons for wanting to – a process known as an exit interview – you may be able to identify ways of reducing turnover and saving money.

Summing up

Staffing and management arrangements will play an important part in achieving the objectives of your business plan. You should start to plan for your organisation's staff requirements by identifying the skills you need and decide how to obtain the necessary skills. It is essential that your plan describes clearly how you will allocate key tasks between different people and how these tasks will be co-ordinated. Your business plan should describe the management structure of your organisation and include details of how you plan to motivate and appraise staff.

Exercises

1   List the skills your organisation will need to achieve the objectives set out in your business plan. In what areas does your organisation need to develop its skills? How do you plan to improve the skills of your organisation in each of these areas?

2   Can you say for certain who in your organisation is responsible for key tasks such as administration, financial management, personnel and marketing?

3   How are the activities of your organisation co-ordinated? Are there any ways in which the co-ordination of activities could be improved?

4   Draw an organisation chart for your organisation. Looking at the chart, can you think of any changes to the management structure of your organisation that would make it more effective?

5   How does your organisation appraise the peformance of its staff? Can you identify any ways in which current systems of appraisal could be improved?

Chapter 8
Financial Planning and Control

This chapter explains how to prepare, and what should be included in, a set of financial projections. It also emphasises the importance of being clear about the assumptions being made when preparing forecasts, and sets out how to design and prepare financial reports.

Preparing financial projections

The preparation of financial projections is often the most daunting part of the business planning process. It involves making assumptions about factors, such as the level of grant income, that may be very uncertain. The fact that funders and management committees will scrutinise your financial plans closely adds extra pressure to get your projections right.

In this chapter we will outline a four-step approach to preparing financial projections that will help you through this process. Once you have practised this approach you will feel more confident about preparing financial forecasts. The four steps are

- Step 1 – the identification of the 'inputs' of your financial projections. These inputs will be all the items such as grant income, salaries, etc, for which you will need information in order to prepare a financial projection for your organisation.

- Step 2 – making assumptions about each of the inputs you have identified. For example, about the size of your grant income or the cost of renting your premises.

- Step 3 – using these assumptions to prepare a set of financial 'outputs' such as a budget for your organisation's income and expenditure.

- Step 4 – completing a 'sensitivity analysis' of the assumptions you have used to prepare your projections. As we saw on p. 27 a sensitivity analysis involves reviewing key assumptions and measuring the impact of changes in those assumptions.

Financial projections – 'inputs'

The inputs to your financial projections are the income and expenditure items for which you will need information to prepare financial forecasts. They will also include indicators of the take-up of your services for activities where increased levels of usage will influence income and expenditure. If, for example, your organisation runs training courses for which it charges a fee, then your income from the courses will depend on how many times they are run and on how many people attend each course.

Below is a checklist of the inputs you will need to list as the first step in preparing your financial projections.

Checklist of inputs

Income	Grants, service level agreements, and contracts
	Income generation activities, eg training courses, publications, etc
	Membership fees

	Donations, legacies, etc
	Prices for courses, publications, other services
Cost/expenditure	Salaries, rent and rates, telephone, heat and light, insurance, marketing and promotion, recruitment, postage and stationery, equipment, repairs and maintenance, travel, professional fees, training, publications, etc
Service take-up	Numbers of users, attendance at training courses, sales of publications, requests for advice, etc

You should review the checklist and add any items that reflect the particular circumstances of your own organisation. A selection of input items also appear in the left-hand column of Table 15 which illustrates the preparation of financial projections for an advice agency.

Making assumptions

The second step in preparing your financial projections involves making assumptions about each of the inputs you have identified. Making assumptions involves three main activities:

- detailing the levels of each income and expenditure item in the current year;

- reviewing the factors that will change the level of income and expenditure in the next year; and

- estimating the amount of change that will take place in each input you have listed.

To complete these activities you should answer the following questions:

1 Will the value of income and expenditure items rise or fall during the next year? For example, will your grants be frozen or cut?

2 By what amount will each item rise or fall? What will the level of your grant income actually be, for instance?

3 What factors explain the estimates you are making of the rise or fall in income and expenditure items? For example, a cut in your grant may be explained by a change in the funding policy of funders.

4 Will the level of demand for your services rise or fall in the next year and by how much? You may estimate that there will be a 20 per cent increase in the number of people seeking your help, for example.

5 How do you know whether the demand for your services will change? The increase in people seeking your help could be explained by a cut in a statutory service.

It is when you come to explaining or even defending your financial projections that the assumptions you have made will be of most use. Think carefully before you answer each question and write down the reasons for your answers so you can refer to them at a later date. It is essential that your assumptions are realistic. You should not make over optimistic estimates in order to impress funders or your management committee. In order to test just how realistic your assumptions are, you should ask a colleague or friend to read your assumptions and to ask you questions about your reasoning.

The process of making assumptions is illustrated in the case study on 'Making Financial Assumptions' and in Table 15.

Case study – making financial assumptions

Downing Advice Centre
Downing Advice Centre provides advice on housing, legal and other issues for local people and community groups. Since it was established in 1975 the Centre has developed a range of other

services in addition to advice. These include training courses for advice workers, a series of publications and an information database for community groups and other advice agencies. As these services have developed, the task of financial planning and control has become increasingly complex. As he sat down to prepare financial projections for 1993 the Centre's director, Edmund Joseph, felt that a new approach was required. 'I need to find a clearer way of presenting our finances to both funders and my committee', he concluded.

The first step he took was to list all the possible items such as rent and heating for which he thought information was needed. The list he made is shown in the left-hand column of Table 15. Next he wrote figures against each of the items on his list. For the three advice workers employed by the Centre, for example, he wrote down details of current salary levels.

In order to review the changes likely in 1993 Edmund invited the chair of his management committee to discuss her views over lunch. For some items such as salaries and rents it was easy to estimate next year's figures. The next rent review was not until 1994 and the project had agreed to increase staff pay by 5 per cent in 1993. Other items such as the likely rise in telephone charges were less easy to estimate. Together the chair and director worked out some figures they felt were reasonable and added them to those in Table 15.

The latest word from the local authority grants unit was that budget difficulties would result in a freeze in grants to all local voluntary organisations. Downing's arrangement with its other main supporter, a local charitable trust, meant a reduction of 10 per cent in its grant for 1993. On a more positive note the Centre's training courses had been so popular during the current year that both the chair and director felt confident that they could put on an extra three courses in 1993. The chair also felt that the course fee could be increased by £10 without reducing interest in the course.

With agreement on the changes likely in 1993 the director

could make his assumptions for the year ahead. Edmund felt
sure that the projections he was now ready to produce would be
the best prepared yet.

There are two further considerations you should keep in mind when
making your financial assumptions:

1   You should state clearly what the figures you are providing
    include. For example, the figures you give for salaries should
    include the cost of paying national insurance and any superannua-
    tion that is payable, or you will underestimate the bill for salaries.

2   You should also make a note of when income and expenditure will
    occur. If, for instance, your organisation pays its salaries on a
    monthly basis but will not receive its first grant cheque until the
    third month of the year, then it is possible that you may run out of
    money before your grant arrives. We will discuss, below, how to
    prepare a cash flow forecast that will show how you have planned
    for any such problems.

Financial projections – 'outputs'

The principal 'outputs' of your financial projections will be budgets
that will help you plan and control the activities of your organisation.
A budget is simply a prepared estimate of future financial events and,
using the financial assumptions you have made, you should prepare
budgets for the following:

- *income and expenditure*   This will enable you to estimate the
  surplus or deficit your organisation will have.

- *cash flow*   This will indicate how much money your organisation
  will have at the end of the year and when any cash problems are
  likely to occur.

To prepare an income and expenditure budget you should list figures
for all the items of income and expenditure you have identified, and

then add each list of figures to produce an estimate for total income and total expenditure. If total income is greater than total expenditure, then you will have a budget surplus. If, however, total expenditure is greater than total income you will be facing a budget deficit.

Table 15   Financial Projections – Downing Advice Centre

'Input' items	Figures for 1992	Changes likely in 1993	Assumptions for 1993
Salaries			
Director	£16,000	Pay up by 5%	£16,800
3 Advisers	£36,000	Pay up by 5%	£37,800
Rent and rates	£7,500	No review till 1994	£7,500
Telephone, heat and light	£6,000	Charges up 3% No change in use	£6,180
Post and stationery	£1,750	Charges up 10%	£1,925
Marketing	£2,500	New leaflet needed	£2,000
Travel	£400	No change	£400
Computer equipment	£1,800	No new purchases	£0
Local authority grant	£43,000	Frozen due to budget crisis	£43,000
Charitable trusts	£19,000	Agreed 10% taper	£17,100
Donations	£6,500	Probably up	£7,000
Training courses	5	Additional 3	8
Training fee	£65	Up by £10	£75
Average course attendance	15	No change	15
Training income	£4,875	Up by £4,125	£9,000
Publications	£1,500	No increase	£1,500

Case study – income and expenditure budget

Downing Advice Centre

Using the figures he had estimated the director prepared the first draft of his income and expenditure budget for 1993. He estimated the Centre's income would be £77,600 and that expenditure would total £72,605. On these figures the Centre could expect to have a surplus during 1993.

Table 16   Draft Income and Expenditure Budget – Downing Advice Centre (£)

Income	
Grants	60,100
Training courses	9,000
Donations	7,000
Publications	1,500
Total Income	77,600
Expenditure	
Salaries	54,600
Rent and rates	7,500
Telephone, heat, light	6,180
Post and stationery	1,925
Marketing and travel	2,400
Total Expenditure	72,605
Estimated budget surplus	4,995

The income and expenditure budget, therefore, tells us both how much income your organisation will receive and how much it will spend during the year. It does not, however, tell us when your income will arrive nor when you will have to pay items such as salary or rent. The income and expenditure budget cannot, therefore, tell if your organisation will experience a shortage of cash during the year. In order to know this you need a cash flow budget.

A cash flow budget details exactly when during the year income will be received and expenditure made. A form for preparing a cash flow budget is provided in Figure 4. Each month of the year is listed along the top of the form and all the income and expenditure items are listed

Figure 4 Cash Flow Pro Forma

Month	January	February	March	April	May	June	July	August	September	October	November	December
Opening balance												
Cash in												
Grants												
Donations												
Other income												
Total in												
Salaries												
Telephone, heat & light												
Other expenses												
Total out												
Net cash flow												
Closing balance												

along the left-hand side of the form. Two other terms used on the form should be noted – opening balance and closing balance. The opening balance indicates how much money your organisation has in its accounts at the start of each month. The closing balance tells you how much is left in those accounts at the end of each month. For example, you start the year with £2,000 in the bank. In January you spend £4,000 and receive £2,000 in grant income. Your expenditure has exceeded income by £2,000 during the month and the closing balance at the end of January will be zero. The closing balance for January automatically becomes the opening balance for February.

To complete the cash flow forecast you need to estimate when you will receive income and make expenditure and then enter the information on the form. For some items this will be straightforward. Salaries, for example, will be paid in equal amounts each month and payment of rent and rates will be either monthly or quarterly. Information on the timing of grant payments will also be readily available. For other items, however, you will have to make assumptions about payments and receipts. One option is to assume that income or expenditure is evenly distributed across the year. You would then divide the total figures by 12 and enter the result for each month on the form. A second option is to look at your records for the past year and see when payments for certain items were due. Telephone bills, for example, will be due four times a year.

Case study – preparing a cash flow forecast

Downing Advice Centre
Before sending his management committee copies of his income and expenditure budget the director remembered what he had learnt on a course on budgeting – only a cash flow forecast would tell him when the Centre might face a shortage of money. He decided to have a go at preparing such a forecast for the Centre and his efforts are reproduced in Figure 5.

Checking the Centre's bank statements the director estimated that the Centre would have £3,500 in the bank at the start of the

Figure 5 Downing Advice Centre Cash Flow Forecast 1993

Month	Jan	Feb	Mar	April	May	June	July	Aug	Sep	Oct	Nov	Dec
Opening balance	3500	52.91	−3394.2	488.73	14142	10695	14577	11130	7682.9	11566	8118.9	4672
Cash in												
Grants			10750	17100		10750			10750			10750
Donations	588.33	588.33	588.33	588.33	588.33	588.33	588.33	588.33	588.33	588.33	588.33	588.33
Other income	875	875	875	875	875	875	875	875	875	875	875	875
Total	1463.3	1463.3	12213	18563	1463.3	12213	1463.3	1463.3	12213	1463.3	1463.3	12213
Cash out												
Salaries	4550	4550	4550	4550	4550	4550	4550	4550	4550	4550	4550	4550
Rent/rates			1875			1875			1875			1875
Telephone heat, etc			1545			1545			1545			1545
Other items	360.42	360.42	360.42	360.42	360.42	360.42	360.42	360.42	360.42	360.42	360.42	360.42
Total	4910.4	4910.4	8330.4	4910.4	4910.4	8330.4	4910.4	4910.4	8330.4	4910.4	4910.4	8330.4
Net cashflow	−3447.1	−3447.1	3882.9	13653	−3447.1	3882.9	−3447.1	−3447.1	3882.9	−3447.1	−3447.1	3882.9
Closing balance	52.91	−3394.2	488.73	14142	10695	14577	11130	7682.9	11566	8118.9	4672	8554.6

year. He duly entered this figure as the opening balance. From the letters setting out the Centre's grant conditions he knew that the local trust would pay all its grant in April and that the local authority would pay its grant in four equal instalments of £10,750 in March, June, September and December.

On donations and other income the director decided that it was best to assume that the money arrived in equal monthly amounts. On average, therefore, donations would be £583.33 a month and other income from training and publications would be £875 a month.

On the expenditure side salaries were paid monthly and represented a regular payment of £4,550. The director checked the Centre's records for the last year and noted that rent, rates and other items including telephone were all paid four times a year. On this basis he assumed four equal payments of these items in March, June, September and December. For the remaining items including marketing and travel the director assumed there would be 12 equal payments of £360.42.

After entering and adding all the figures on the cash flow form he had been given on the training course, the director noted that the Centre would have over £8,500 in the bank at the end of the year (Figure 5). More worryingly, the forecast showed that the Centre would run out of cash in February and would not be able to meet any more payments until the grant cheque arrived from the Council. In order for the Centre to pay its staff's wages during February either the director would have to arrange an overdraft with the Centre's bank or he would have to see if the Centre could receive an advance payment of grant.

The clear implication of the cash flow analysis illustrated in the case study on 'Preparing a Cash Flow Forecast' is that your organisation may, at some point in the year, run out of money to pay bills and salaries even though the budget shows that you will end the year with a surplus. In Downing's case the cash flow problems would have been even worse if – as is often the case in the real world – its grant payments were late. There are three basic rules to follow to minimise the extent of cash flow problems:

1 Attempt to get those organisations who owe you money to pay as early as possible. Downing's cash flow problems would have been avoided if they could have persuaded the local authority to make an advance grant payment in February.

2 Pay organisations to whom you owe money at the last possible moment that is consistent with the payment terms they have set. It may also be possible to negotiate more favourable terms with your suppliers.

3 If you anticipate that you will need an overdraft from your bank, negotiate it while you still have money in the bank. If you are already in the middle of a cash flow crisis the bank will be less likely to agree an overdraft and will probably charge you more for it.

Presenting your financial projections

Before we consider how to test the assumptions on which your financial projections are based it is important to think about how best to present the 'outputs' of your financial analysis. Your projections should be presented in a way that

- shows the relationship between the assumptions you have made and the budgets that result from those assumptions;

- facilitates a sensitivity analysis of your financial assumptions; and

- looks neat and professional to the reader of your plan.

The best way to achieve these presentation aims is to set out your assumptions at the top of the page and then detail the budget that results underneath. An example of such a presentation is given in Table 17.

Table 17   Presentation of Financial Projections

Assumptions

Number of staff	2	Grants	£35,000
Salaries	£15,000	Donations	£5,500
Rent and rates	£5,000	Other income	£2,700
Other costs	£8,600		

Income and expenditure budget

Income (£)

Grants	35,000
Donations	5,500
Other	2,700
Total	43,200

Expenditure (£)

Salaries	30,000
Rent and rates	5,000
Other costs	8,600
Total	43,600
Deficit	400

The figures in the table are very clearly laid out and it is easy to see from the assumptions made how the budget deficit of £400 has been estimated. We can also change a key assumption and see how it affects the budget. If, for example, we assume that grants will be £37,000 instead of £35,000 then income will rise by £2,000 to £45,200 and the organisation will have a budget surplus of £1,600.

Completing a sensitivity analysis

The process of changing a key financial assumption and measuring the effect of the change on the budget forecast is known as sensitivity analysis. There are three main reasons why you should complete such an analysis of your financial assumptions:

1 Your financial plans should reflect the fact that your organisation's environment is uncertain and changing. By reviewing your assumptions you are taking into account the possibility and effect of such change on your finances.

2 We have seen that budgets are very dependent on the assumptions you make. A sensitivity analysis will test your reasons for making those assumptions and should give your forecast more authority.

3 The review of assumptions will help you prepare for events that may influence your finances. A sensitivity analysis will help you identify those events that are likely to have the biggest effect on your organisation and to prepare the actions you will take to cope if they happen.

The best way to illustrate a sensitivity analysis is to look at the Downing Advice Centre again.

Case study – sensitivity analysis

Downing Advice Centre
The director of the Centre sent his financial forecasts to each member of the management committee for comment and, after a few days, comments started to arrive. While the committee were pleasantly surprised at the budget surplus that was forecast, a number of concerns were expressed about the assumptions on which the forecast was based. To the director these concerns seemed to be about three key assumptions:

1 *the level of grant from the local authority* Some members of the committee felt that the director was being over optimistic in assuming that the grant would be at the same level as in 1992. It might be more advisable, they suggested, to assume a cut in the grant of anything up to 15 per cent.

2 *the demand for the Centre's training courses* The overwhelming view was that, in this case, the director had erred in the opposite direction. It was felt that he was too cautious

in estimating the potential to increase the number of courses provided and the price that was charged for attending the course.

3 *the level of donations that the Centre would receive* The continuing recession led most members of the committee to suggest that donations were more likely to fall than to rise as had been assumed by the director.

As he reflected on the comments the director thought that what was needed was a means of illustrating the effects on the forecast budget of changes in his original assumptions. He had heard about sensitivity analysis and decided to try the technique for himself. The result of his analysis, which is shown below, would form the basis of a report to the next meeting of the management committee.

Table 18 Income and Expenditure Forecast: Sensitivity Analysis – Downing Advice Centre

Assumption	Change in assumption	Effect on budget forecast
Local authority grant	10% cut	£4,300 worse
	15% cut	£6,450 worse
Training courses	2 extra	£2,250 better
	Increase price to £85	£1,200 better
Donations	10% lower than forecast	£700 worse
	25% lower than forecast	£1,750 worse

The director's analysis helped him to some important conclusions. The biggest worry for the organisation would be a cut in the grant. Even a fairly large fall in donations would be less damaging than a small cut in the grant. If the Centre wanted to earn more income from its training courses, it would be better to increase the number of courses run rather than increase the price. In any case the director believed that to increase the price further would drive away the advice workers who wanted to come on the course.

Financial reporting

In addition to making financial forecasts your business plan should also show how you intend to monitor and control the finances of your organisation. For this you will need a financial reporting system that

- compares the actual income and expenditure of your organisation with the figures in your budget;

- enables you to explain any differences between actual and budget figures; and

- helps you identify appropriate management action in response to figures that are worse than those for which you budgeted,

A form for preparing such a report is provided in Figure 6. The form provides space to compare actual income and expenditure with the amounts estimated in your budget. The difference between these figures is known as the variance. If, for example, actual income is higher than budget income then you will have a positive variance. If, however, actual income is lower than budget income then you will have a negative variance.

The fourth column on the form is headed 'Explanation for variance'. In this column you should explain why actual and budgeted figures differ. Actual income may be lower than budget because of a late grant payment or because donations are lower than expected, for example. The most important variances are those that are large in size because it is these that are likely to require management action. For example, if actual expenditure on telephones and postage is exceeding budget figures, then you may propose ways of reducing expenditure such as greater use of second class post or restricting the use of telephones to times of the day when cheaper rates are available.

The form is suitable for regular use by managers and for making reports to management committees. You should indicate in your business plan how often you will fill in the form and who will be responsible for taking any recommended action. As a rule of thumb you should prepare financial reports on a monthly basis so that you become aware of any budget problems before it is too late to identify corrective action.

The form in Figure 6 can be extended to provide a more detailed analysis of the income and expenditure associated with the different activities of your organisation. The starting-point for a more detailed analysis is the identification of cost centres. Cost centres are individual activities or sections of your organisation, eg training, advice, publications, etc for which income and expenditure are separately identifiable.

One voluntary organisation that uses cost centre reporting is the International Health Exchange (IHE). It decided to record income and expenditure for four of its activities and then to compare the financial performance of each activity. As a result of the analysis IHE concluded that the income from one activity – the conduct, on behalf of overseas development charities, of searches for health personnel – was disappointing. As a result extra administrative support was found and more emphasis given to finding people who met the needs of client organisations. Since these changes were made the number of appointments arranged by IHE has risen and so too has the organisation's income.

The major benefit of cost centre reporting, therefore, is the help it will give you in identifying the financial contribution that each centre makes to your organisation. A form for preparing a cost centre report simply requires replacing the row titled 'Total surplus/deficit' in the form provided in Figure 6. The new row, which is titled 'Contribution', shows the actual surplus or deficit from the activity of an individual cost centre. Preparing cost centre reports for each activity will enable you to compare how much each contributes to the central or 'overhead' costs of your organisation. Overhead costs are those costs, such as rent or insurance, that are not directly related to the individual activities of each cost centre. If the total contribution from

Figure 6   Financial Reporting Pro Forma

	Actual	Budget	Variance	Explanation for variance
Income				
Expenditure				
Total surplus/deficit				
Recommended management action				

Figure 7   Cost Centre Reporting Pro Forma

Identity of cost centre	Actual	Budget	Variance	Explanation for variance
Income				
Expenditure				
Contribution				
Recommended management action				

cost centre activities is equal to the value of overheads then your organisation will avoid a deficit. A pro forma for a cost centre report is given in Figure 7.

Summing Up

In preparing financial projections for your business plan you should follow four main steps. Firstly, you will need to identify the inputs, such as grant income and salary costs, that you will need to include in your projections. Secondly, you should state what your assumptions are about each of these inputs. Using your assumptions you should then prepare financial forecasts for the period ahead. You should prepare forecasts for both income and expenditure and for cash flow. Finally, you should test the assumptions you have used to prepare your financial projections by the means of a sensitivity analysis.

Your business plan should also provide information on the financial reporting system the organisation will use to monitor and control its finances.

Exercises

1   Following the checklist on pp. 87–8 make a list of the 'inputs' for which you will need information in order to prepare your financial projections.

2   For the year ahead, what are your assumptions about each of the inputs you have identified?

3   What would be the impact on Downing Advice Centre's draft income and expenditure budget (p. 93) of each of the following:

(a)   donations are 50 per cent lower than forecast

(b)   a freeze in the pay of staff

(c)   a 5 per cent *increase* in the local authority grant

(d)   an increase in the fees charged for its training courses to £85 per person

4 A cash flow forecast for the Downing Advice Centre is provided on p. 96. Prepare a revised cash flow forecast that takes account of *both* of the following:

- local authority grant payments are received one month later than originally anticipated

- 'other' income is 20 per cent higher than anticipated

What is the new opening balance for April? What is the Centre's closing balance in December?

Suggested answers to Exercises 3 and 4 are provided in Appendix 1.

5 Summarise the workings of your current systems for financial reporting. What are its strengths and weaknesses? What changes, if any, do you think are necessary?

Chapter 9
Preparing and Presenting the Business Plan

This chapter discusses how best to present the organisation's business plan. It considers the overall structure, where to discuss key issues and the needs of the different audiences for the plan.

After the analysis, discussion and research of the preceding stages of the business planning process you should now be ready to write and present your plan.

Writing your plan

It is likely that, when you come to write up your plan, you will have a large amount of information to consider and organise. It is essential that you approach the task of writing it with two aims in mind:

- to organise the material in a clearly structured document; and

- to ensure that the plan is consistent. That is, you should aim to make sure that different parts of your plan, such as those on staffing and finance, do not contradict each other.

You will find it easier to achieve these two objectives if you adopt the following approach:

1   Decide first on a structure for the first draft of your business plan. We will discuss an outline structure in detail, below, but it is likely that the plan will begin with an executive summary and conclude with a section on finance.

2   In writing the plan, follow the steps you have taken in the business planning process. You should start, therefore, with a discussion of your objectives and services. This will be followed by a summary of the opportunities and threats facing your organisation, and then by sections (on marketing, staffing, finance, etc) that indicate how you will implement the plan. It is generally not a good idea to start by writing up your financial projections and then working back to other sections such as marketing. This will distort the focus of your plan and result in financial projections which do not reflect your objectives and service priorities. It is much better to detail your plans, and how you will implement them, and then acknowledge the financial constraints you face in the financial section itself.

   The one exception to this guidance on writing up your plan is the executive summary. Although this will appear at the front of your business plan it should be the last section to be written. In this way it will reflect the contents of the plan itself.

3   Prepare a draft version of your business plan and then review its contents. In particular you should consider whether:

   • there are any significant gaps that should be filled;

   • it clearly expresses your organisation's plans and priorities;

   • it gives a convincing account of how your plans will be carried out; and

   • the contents of different sections of the plan are consistent with each other.

   Now would also be a good time to consult with staff and management committee members about your plan. This will help you revise the content of the plan and help establish the sense of ownership which is necessary for successful implementation. A short guide to the evaluation of your business plan is included in Appendix 2.

4 Finally, prepare a revised version of your business plan and present it to your management team or committee for approval and adoption.

The structure of your plan

The structure that you choose for your business plan should be customised to the particular needs of your organisation. Your final written plan should reflect the importance of different activities, such as marketing or staff development, to the achievement of your objectives. While no two business plans will be organised in exactly the same way it is possible to suggest an outline structure which will help you in organising your material and thoughts.

Suggested headings for each section of your business plan are set out in Table 19. The outline structure shown in the table consists of eight main sections followed by appendices. The detailed content of each suggested section is discussed below.

Table 19   Structure of a Business Plan

Section	Heading
One	Executive summary
Two	Background and history
Three	Service profile
Four	Environmental analysis
Five	Marketing strategy
Six	Operations
Seven	Staffing and management
Eight	Finance
Appendices	

Executive summary

Written after the other sections the executive summary should summarise the contents of your plan. Along with the sections on staffing and finance it is the section that will be most closely read by prospective funders. It should, therefore, be written in a way that makes the reader interested in, and positive towards, your organisation. To achieve this you should be brief – this section of your plan should be no longer than two sides of A4 paper – and clear.

The section should begin with a clear summary of:

- the fundamental purpose or mission of your organisation

- the needs or demands that you hope to meet

- those factors that make it likely that your organisation will be successful in realising its aims (see p. 26)

These details should win the attention of the reader and give them a picture of what your organisation does and hopes to achieve.

This should be followed by a short summary of the content of each of the remaining sections. At the end of your executive summary you should briefly indicate how you intend to take the plan forward, eg by the preparation of an implementation plan.

Background and history

In this section you should describe the philosophy or mission of your organisation in more detail. You should list the principal objectives of your organisation and describe its past record and current position. This section should, for example, detail when and how your organisation came into being, and should list important milestones in its development. If you are writing a business plan for a new project, this section should provide information on the background and history of the idea or objectives for the new organisation.

In many business plans this section is entitled 'Mission and Objectives' or 'Position Statement', both of which reflect the status of this section as a description of where the organisation currently is in its development.

Service profile

In this section you should provide a detailed description of the services and activities that will enable your organisation to achieve its aims. For each service or activity you should provide the following:

- a description of the service or activity and of the users for whom they are intended;

- a description of how the service or activity will be developed during the period of your business plan;

- details of performance targets and desired service outcomes (see p. 24); and

- a brief summary of the implications of your service plans for marketing, personnel, operations and finance. You should confirm at this point that these implications will be discussed in more detail in subsequent sections of your plan.

An illustration of what an individual service profile might look like is given below.

Service Profile

Service area	Training courses
Service range	Courses for other voluntary organisations in managing contracts with funders
	New courses to be developed and offered in costing contracts and in negotiation skills
Targets and outcomes	Current courses – 50 participants; 80 per cent rating course as 'very useful' or 'quite useful'
	New courses – 30 participants; 70 per cent rating courses as 'very useful' or 'quite useful'
Implications for the organisation	*Marketing* – concentrate on advertising, mailing of course programme, and letters to previous clients
	Human resources – allocation of additional staff resources to promotion

> *Operations* – apply for external validation of courses
> *Finance* – seek external finance or subsidy to enable
> courses to be offered to more people

Environmental analysis

This section, which might also be entitled 'The Environment', should contain a brief summary of the environmental analysis you have conducted (see Chapter 4). The summary should concentrate on the implications of the analysis for your own organisation. For example, your analysis might show that there is a need for your organisation to raise both its profile and awareness among potential users of its services. Or your analysis may have identified a major opportunity for your organisation to acquire new sources of finance if its opening hours could be extended.

It may help the readers of your plan to understand your organisation's environment if you present your analysis in the form of a diagram. An example of such a diagram is provided in Figure 8. It portrays the organisation in the middle and the most important trends and influences (legislation, funding, etc) surrounding it. You could extend the diagram by showing the linkages between individual environmental factors, eg between government legislation on community care and the funding policies of your principal funders.

You should conclude your environmental analysis with a summary SWOT analysis (see pp. 42–3) and a positioning statement (see p. 53) that summarises how you intend to respond to the opportunities your analysis has identified. The rest of your business plan will provide readers with detailed information on how you intend to maximise opportunities and minimise the impact of threats.

Marketing strategy

This section should begin with a brief summary of your organisation's current marketing activity. This should be followed by a description of your organisation's marketing objectives and an indication of which objectives are priorities over the period of your business plan. You should then specify the individuals and organisations that will be the targets for your marketing activity, the process of segmentation (see p. 51).

Figure 8   Presentation of an Environmental Analysis

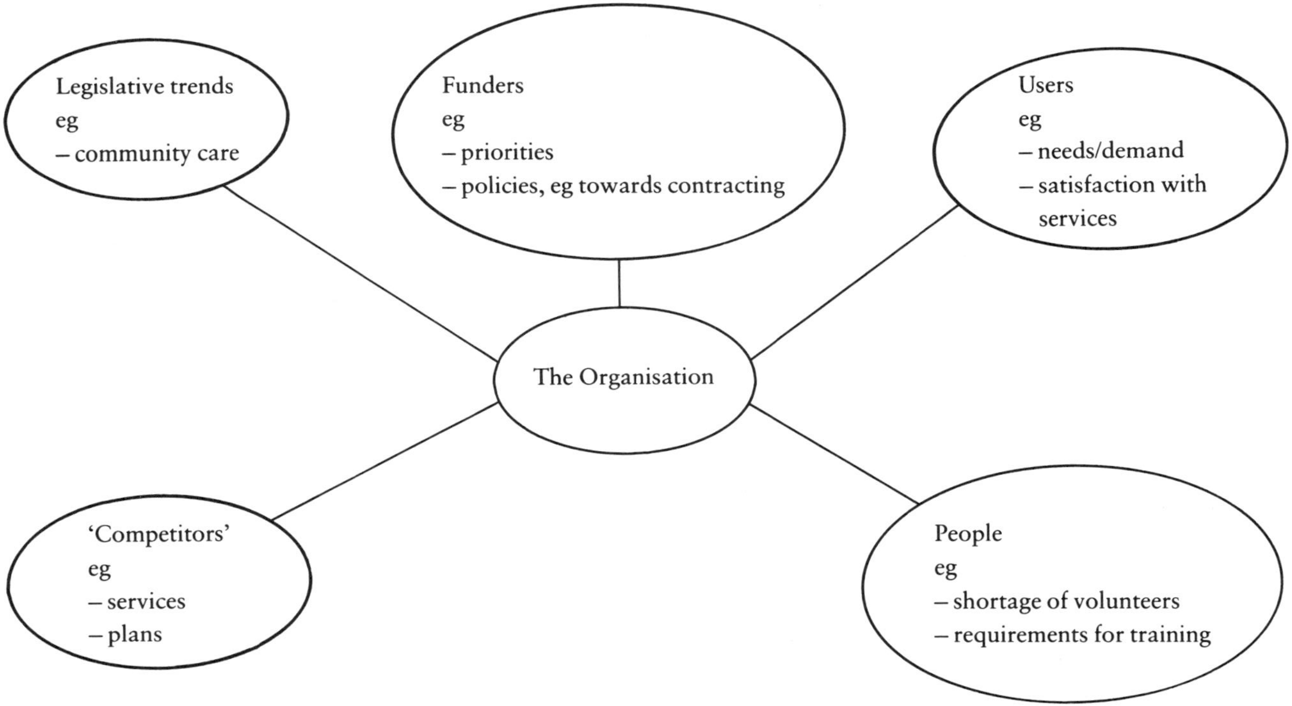

The Organisation

Users
eg
– needs/demand
– satisfaction with services

People
eg
– shortage of volunteers
– requirements for training

Funders
eg
– priorities
– policies, eg towards contracting

Legislative trends
eg
– community care

'Competitors'
eg
– services
– plans

The most important part of this section will be the details of the mix of marketing tools you plan to use in order to achieve your marketing objectives. You should describe your proposed marketing activity, eg giving details of where you will advertise or how you will make your premises more accessible to users. You may find it helpful to summarise your selection of marketing tools with a diagram such as that of Figure 2 on p. 47.

The marketing section of your business plan will be completed by the inclusion of the details of implementation. This will include the specification of a budget for marketing and procedures for keeping marketing information and reviewing the effects of your strategy.

Operations

In this section you are aiming to show you have considered the operational requirements of your plan and that you will be able to manage effectively. The content and importance of this section will vary considerably between different organisations. In one voluntary organisation operational issues, such as capacity management, were so important that they were discussed with services in an extensive section entitled 'Service Management and Operations'. In most cases, however, operational issues can be considered in a separate section.

This section will include the results of your work on the issues discussed in Chapter 6. Thus it will cover:

- the roles of people and equipment in delivering services

- a description of your management information systems

- a description of how you intend to monitor and evaluate your activities, and ensure a high quality of service

- a discussion of any legal issues and of the suitability of your organisation's premises

Staffing and management

People hold the key to the ultimate success of your business plan. This section of your plan should describe the staffing and management structure of the organisation. It should indicate how you will develop the skills necessary for success through recruitment and staff training, and how you intend to tap the skills and energy of volunteers and management committee members. You should also describe how you plan to reward and motivate staff, providing information on any systems of staff appraisal.

It is important that in this section you are clear about the lines of authority and responsibility. An organisation chart will help readers to understand how activity is co-ordinated. You should also provide biographies or CVs of key staff. You may also want to include details of other personnel systems used by your organisation and to set out staffing objectives such as a target for staff turnover.

Finance

The main objective of this section of your plan is to provide a clear overview of your organisation's financial position for the period covered by the plan. You should start with some 'financial highlights', a summary of projected income and expenditure with a commentary on significant trends and financing issues. For example, you may need to highlight the need to raise additional funds to meet a projected deficit. Your financial highlights should also include a commentary on the cash flow analysis you have completed, discussing any likely problems and indicating how the organisation will manage any difficulties.

It is not necessary to include a lot of detail here. You should refer the reader to supporting information in the appendices (see below). Altogether this section should be no more than three to four pages of A4 paper. You should, however, include details of the key assumptions upon which your financial projections are based and show the results of the sensitivity analysis you have completed. Finally this section of your plan should include a brief description of the systems you will use to monitor and control the finances of your organisation.

Appendices

The appendices to your business plan should contain documentation in support of the plan's contents. What you decide to include in the appendices depends to a large extent on what you think the readers of your plan might require. It is likely, however, that the appendices will include:

- detailed information on the financial assumptions that shaped the financial highlights in section eight of your plan;

- copies of questionnaires used by your organisation to conduct an environmental analysis together with information on the number or identity of people interviewed;

- an analysis of the findings of 'market research' conducted for the plan; and

- detailed specifications for premises or equipment.

You may also want to include a programme or plan for implementing your business plan in the appendices. We shall discuss implementation plans in Chapter 10.

Presenting your plan

The way in which you present your business plan will determine whether it is actually read by important audiences and the reaction these readers will have to its contents. We will discuss some presentation objectives for business plans below, but there are three general areas of presentation which require your attention:

1 *layout* Your plan should have a cover page which details the name of your organisation, the period covered by the business plan, and provide information on how a reader can make contact. This should be followed by a detailed contents page. You should regard the contents page as a map which guides readers to the sections in which they are interested. It should, therefore, contain plenty of numbered sub-headings, eg 5.3 Marketing Mix, and references to the number of the page on which section and sub-section starts. Sub-headings will also help break up the text and make it easier for readers to follow the logic of your plan.

2 *length* We are often asked how long a business plan should be. Since every plan will be unique this is a difficult question. In general, however, business plans should be no longer than 25 pages of A4 paper in length. Aiming for this length as a target will prove a useful discipline when it comes to writing your plan.

3 *checking of spelling and grammar*   Your business plan will be one
of the ways in which you present your organisation to the outside
world. You want it to be accurate and professional. If possible,
therefore, you should ask someone to check it for spelling or other
mistakes. You should also double check that figures included in the
business plan add up.

Presentation objectives

In addition to the general points, above, you should follow six
presentation objectives when preparing your business plan.

1 *Your business plan should contain appropriate messages for its
different audiences.* There will be two main audiences for your
business plan. An 'internal' audience consisting of staff, managers
and management committee members, and an 'external' audience
consisting largely of funders. To the internal audience you should
aim to convey a sense of direction and organisational purpose. To
the external audience you should try to convey a sense of your
organisation's viability, of its likelihood of success.

We are often asked whether the needs of different audiences can
be catered for within just one business planning document. In most
cases it should be possible to adjust the text to take account of
different readers. It may be a good idea, however, to produce
different versions of your plan for its respective audiences. For the
external audience, for example, you may wish to concentrate more
on your financial projections, marketing plans and management
arrangements. For the internal audience you may decide to focus
on those issues (objectives, service development, etc) that reinforce
commitment to your organisation. Ultimately this is a judgement
for you, with specific knowledge of the needs of your internal and
external audiences, to make. Preparing your business plan on a
word processor will, however, save considerable time if you do
decide to produce more than one version of your plan.

2 *You should aim to be as clear as possible in expressing the contents
of your plan.* It is essential that your plans and objectives are
clearly expressed. It is particularly important that the reader is
clear about the aims of your organisation, about the need for your

services and about those factors that will make your organisation a success.

3 *You should present your business plan in a concise form.* Make sure that it is easy for your readers to find key information. Try to contain your business plan to within 25 pages. Most readers will have neither the time nor inclination to read plans that are much longer than this.

4 *Write your plan in such a way that it is easy to prepare a verbal presentation of its main points.* You should be able to extract material for a 10-minute verbal presentation on the contents of your plans. You will be able to do this if you are clear and concise in expression and the layout of your plan makes it possible to identify important points.

5 *Write your plan so that it is easy to implement.* At each stage your business plan should identify implementation tasks and responsibilities, and should set targets that will assist with monitoring and review. We will discuss implementation in more detail in Chapter 10.

6 *Try to make your plan lively and interesting.* It will help if you try to put yourself in the place of a reader. Assume that they have little time to read plans and that many of the plans they receive are long and dull. Think carefully about what will interest them and make your organisation stand out. Make the most of opportunities to personalise your plan. Biographies of key staff is one way. Also you may want to include short profiles of different activities and to illustrate the positive influence of your work on the lives of your users. Despite the unavoidable discussion of finance and systems try to retain the focus on people that will engage the attention of readers.

Summing Up

The content, structure and length of your business plan will depend on the circumstances of your organisation and the needs of different audiences for the plan. There are, however, some guidelines that you should follow when preparing your plan. Above all you should try to make your business plan clear, concise and lively. You will also need to decide whether to produce more than one version of your plan so that it is suitable for different groups of reader.

Exercises

1   Draft an outline structure for your business plan. Under each section heading identify the subjects you intend to cover.

2   Prepare 'financial highlights' as suggested on p. 115. Does the information you have summarised give a clear picture of your organisation's financial needs? Write a commentary that describes the key items of financial information.

3   Make a list of the people who will be reading your business plan and identify what you consider each 'audience' will be looking for from it. Use your observations to decide how many versions of your business plan you will produce.

Chapter 10
Implementing
the Business Plan

This chapter emphasises the importance of having a plan for implementing the business plan and the role of monitoring and evaluation in implementation. It also points out the common pitfalls in implementing business plans and advises on how to avoid them.

Implementation plans

Given the time and effort you have put into preparing the business plan it is important that it becomes a useful working document for your organisation. Ideally your plan should become a source of guidance on how your organisation and its services will develop. The alternative is that your document will, once it has been read and agreed, sit on the shelf in your office and gather dust. Not only will your efforts be wasted but you will have missed an important opportunity to implement the conclusions of your plan.

An implementation plan will represent the first step in ensuring that your plan becomes a useful working document. If you have followed the process outlined in the preceding chapters you will have identified targets and tasks in many areas together with the responsibility for implementation. Your implementation plan will bring all this work together in one document. For each important area in the plan, such as marketing or service development, you should identify the following:

- key implementation tasks

- the responsibility for implementation

- important targets and timescales for their achievement

- the procedures you will use to review progress with implementation, eg quarterly reports, monthly management meetings, etc

A pro forma for the completion of an implementation plan is presented in Figure 9.

You may wish to include an implementation plan as an appendix to your main business plan or decide to prepare a separate document once your business plan has been adopted by your organisation. Either arrangement will serve the central purpose of the plan which is to guide your organisation through the implementation of your business plan.

We will discuss the contribution of monitoring and evaluation to the implementation of your business plan below. Your implementation plan should, however, include monitoring and evaluation as a key implementation task. It should, therefore, identify responsibility for monitoring and evaluation and detail both the timetable and procedures for undertaking monitoring and evaluation work.

Implementation pitfalls

No matter how well you prepare both your business plan and your implementation plan, the implementation process is likely to encounter some difficulties. You should be aware of the common implementation pitfalls you may encounter and the ways in which you can overcome these pitfalls. Eight of the most common implementation pitfalls are listed below together with suggested management responses.

1 *Implementation of your business plan lacks co-ordination.* The dangers of badly co-ordinated activity were highlighted in Chapter

Figure 9 Implementation Plan Pro Forma

Implementation area	Key implementation tasks	Responsibility for key tasks	Targets and timescales	Review process

7. If your implementation process is lacking co-ordination there are three steps you can take:

- Form a team to take responsibility for implementation. The team should include members of staff with responsibility for activities that are central to the achievement of your aims.

- Nominate one person as responsible for overall co-ordination of implementation. It is important that this person should be given sufficient authority to overcome any other obstacles to implementation such as the opposition of individual members of staff, for example.

- Improve communication between your staff on the implementation of the plan. Regular implementation reports or meetings to consider progress are two ways in which better communication can be achieved.

2 *Staff are unable to switch from existing activity to the new tasks required for implementation.* In many organisations staff can be preoccupied with existing tasks and lack either the time or the commitment to switch to new activities that reflect the priorities of a business plan. To overcome this difficulty you should ensure that

- you give a high priority to communicating your organisation's new plans and priorities;

- staff are required to make regular reports on progress with new tasks; and

- you show a strong management lead and give sufficient management time to implementation.

3 *Staff do not understand or accept responsibility for implementing the plan.* The likelihood that you will face this implementation difficulty will be reduced if you have communicated your reasons for producing the plan to your staff and have consulted on its preparation and content. Better communication and consultation are, therefore, two common responses to this pitfall. If persuasion and communication do not work you will have little alternative

but to use your management authority to ensure that implementation takes place.

4   *The financial projections on which your business plan are based are not realised.*   This pitfall could arise from either a shortfall of income, eg as a result of an unexpected cut in your grant, or from over-expenditure, eg on renovating your organisation's premises. You should look at your income and expenditure budgets and consider where expenditure can be cut or new sources of income found. Concentrate your action on income and expenditure items that are both large in size and subject to your control. There is little point, for example, in looking at factors such as rent that you cannot influence in the short run, or at small items of expenditure that make little difference to your overall financial situation. If you are unable to bring your financial projections back into line with your business plan you will need to revise the plan itself.

5   *Management information systems fail to keep up with the needs of implementation.*   The development of new management information systems can be very time-consuming and, for many voluntary organisations who focus on actual service delivery, this development is often much slower than managers would like. Typical problems include

- an absence of clear information on the number and type of enquiries made to an organisation

- insufficient detail on the income and expenditure associated with different activities

- a failure to record how staff are using their time

A number of solutions are available. You could

- Hire specialist support on a temporary basis to establish new systems and train staff in their use.

- Assign specific responsibility for developing new systems to an individual member of staff and require regular reports on progress.

- Consider how existing systems can be modified until there is sufficient time to implement systems proposed in your business plan.

6 *Key staff leave your organisation during the period of the plan.* The loss of key staff can pose a serious threat to the implementation of your plan since it will take time to recruit, induct and train a suitable replacement. You can minimise the effect of the departure of key staff by

- encouraging team work and the sharing of skills and experience;

- training staff in the skills needed to complete key tasks in the event of other staff leaving; and

- planning in advance how you might respond to the departure of such staff. It is a good idea, for example, to keep records of volunteers or outside advisers who might be able to fill any gaps in your organisation while you recruit a new member of staff.

7 *The management committee does not accept or understand the need for implementation of your proposals.* For similar reasons as staff (see above) your management committee may not be convinced of the need to implement the proposals in the business plan. As with staff, improved communication and fuller consultation about your plans will help overcome this pitfall. It will not be possible, however, to use management authority to overcome problems with a management committee. If communication does not work you should try directly asking your committee to support implementation or seek assistance in the form of arbitration from an external agency such as a funder.

8 *Your plans are over ambitious.* In Chapter 3 we discussed the importance of being realistic about the timescales and objectives you set yourself. If you are falling short of your targets you can

- see if you can allocate more time or resources to the tasks necessary to achieve your targets; or

- revise the targets.

In either case you will need to keep targets under constant review.

In Chapter 2 we advised you to think about the problems you would encounter during the business planning process. You should extend this to the problems of implementation since the extent of implementation problems can be reduced by careful pre-planning and anticipation.

The role of monitoring and evaluation

We discussed monitoring and evaluation in more detail in Chapter 6 above (see pp. 66–8 in particular). It is worth summarising their role in the implementation of the business plan. Monitoring and evaluation

- should, as we noted above, be a key activity within your implementation plan;

- will help you keep your performance targets under review and will, therefore, play an important part in measuring whether you are successfully implementing your business plan; and

- will help you identify the key factors, such as user satisfaction with services and finance, that you need to control in order to ensure success as an organisation.

Summing up

An implementation plan will help you ensure that your business plan becomes a useful working document. For each area of activity this plan should identify key implementation tasks and assign responsibility for implementation. It should also set timescales and detail the procedures you will use to monitor progress. A number of common implementation difficulties can be anticipated. The effect these pitfalls will have on your organisation can be reduced or eliminated by careful planning.

Now that you have read the book, and followed the exercises at the end of each chapter, you will be ready to engage in successful business planning. By applying the techniques we have described you will improve your working arrangements and planning for the future. Above all your business plan will help your organisation survive and prosper in the years ahead.

The work you will need to put into preparing your first plan may well be considerable but so will the rewards. Business planning will gradually become an integral part of organisational life and you will develop new skills and confidence. And, with each successive plan, your organisation will be better placed to manage its future successfully.

Exercises

1   Using the form provided in Figure 9, draw up a plan to implement your business plan.

2   Review the timescales you have set for implementation. Will you have sufficient time and resources to achieve these timescales? If not, what action do you plan to take?

3   What implementation pitfalls do you anticipate? For each pitfall identify at least three ways in which you will overcome the problems that result.

Appendix 1

Suggested Answers to Exercises 3 and 4, Chapter 8

Exercise 3

(a) The effect of a 50% fall in forecast donations is to reduce donations to £3,500. The Centre's projected surplus falls to £1,495, a reduction of £3,500.

(b) If staff pay is frozen then it will remain at its levels for 1992. This was £52,000, a figure which is £2,600 less than the original forecast. The projected surplus rises to £7,595.

(c) The grant is currently £43,000 per annum. A 5% increase would take the figure to £45,150 increasing the forecast surplus by £2,150 to £7,145.

(d) A fee of £85 represents an increase per person of £10. The average course attendance is expected to be 15 so the average income per course will be £150 higher (15 multiplied by £10). The Centre plans to run eight courses so the total income from training courses will rise by £1,200 (8 multiplied by £150). The projected surplus will rise to £6,195.

Exercise 4

There will be two main changes to the cash flow forecast.

- grant payments from the local authority will now be received in April, July, October and the January of the year following that for which the forecast is being prepared (ie 1994)

- 'other' income will now be 20% higher at £1,050 a month

Figure 10 Downing Advice Centre Cashflow Forecast 1993

Month	Jan	Feb	Mar	April	May	June	July	Aug	Sep	Oct	Nov	Dec
Opening balance	3500	227.9	−3044.2	−9736.3	14841.6	11569.5	4877.4	12355.3	9083.2	2391.1	9869	6596.9
Cash in												
Grants			0	27850		0	10750		0	10750		0
Donations	588.3	588.3	588.3	588.3	588.3	588.3	588.3	588.3	588.3	588.3	588.3	588.3
Other income	1050	1050	1050	1050	1050	1050	1050	1050	1050	1050	1050	1050
Total	1638.3	1638.3	1638.3	29488.3	1638.3	1638.3	12388.3	1638.3	1638.3	12388.3	1638.3	1638.3
Cash out												
Salaries	4550	4550	4550	4550	4550	4550	4550	4550	4550	4550	4550	4550
Rent/rates			1875			1875			1875			1875
Telephone, heat, etc			1545			1545			1545			1545
Other items	360.4	360.4	360.4	360.4	360.4	360.4	360.4	360.4	360.4	360.4	360.4	360.4
Total	4910.4	4910.4	8330.4	4910.4	4910.4	8330.4	4910.4	4910.4	8330.4	4910.4	4910.4	8330.4
Net cashflow	−3272.1	−3272.1	−6692.1	24577.9	−3272.1	−6692.1	7477.9	−3272.1	−6692.1	7477.9	−3272.1	−6692.1
Closing balance	227.9	−3044.2	−9736.3	14841.6	11569.5	4877.4	12355.3	9083.2	2391.1	9869	6596.9	−95.2

A revised cash flow forecast is set out in Figure 10. It shows that the net effect of the two changes is a significantly worse cash flow than originally forecast. The Centre will start April with a deficit of £9,736.30 and will finish December with a deficit of £95 instead of the cash surplus of over £8,500 which was originally forecast.

Appendix 2

A Short Guide to the Evaluation of Business Plans

This appendix provides a guide, for both managers and funders, to the evaluation of business plans. As a manager in a voluntary organisation you can use the guide to assess the strengths and weaknesses of your business plan and to anticipate the comments of funders who read it. As a funder of voluntary organisations you can use the guide to help you decide whether to invest resources in a particular project or group.

There are four basic steps to the evaluation of a business plan:

- an initial review to assess the organisation's success in communicating its purpose and strengths

- a detailed review of the contents of the business plan

- verification of claims and assumptions made in the business plan

- final assessment of the business plan

Initial review

At this stage you should skim through the business plan focusing mostly on the executive summary and the statement of objectives. Your aim should be to answer some initial, but fundamental, questions about the plan:

1 Does the plan give a clear sense of what the organisation does and why its services and activities are important?

2 On reading the plan do you have a feeling for what the organisation is actually like, for its culture and approach to service delivery?

3   Are you clear what the organisation has got going for it? Do you understand what it is that will make the organisation a success in achieving its short-term objectives and longer-term aims?

If the answers to these initial questions are largely positive then you can conclude that the basic foundation for a successful business plan has been laid. If, however, the answer to these questions is largely negative then it is better to suggest revisions to key statements in the plan before you proceed to a more detailed review of its contents. If the plan is unclear about what an organisation does or why, then it is unlikely that the rest of the plan will convince you that the organisation will achieve its objectives.

Detailed review

The second stage of your evaluation requires you to read the plan in detail from start to finish with three aims in mind:

1   *to enable you to complete an evaluation checklist.*   An evaluation checklist is suggested below. To each group of items or questions on the checklist you should answer yes or no and make a note of any comments that you think would improve the final version.

Business plans: evaluation checklist

Objectives
Are the objectives of the organisation clear, consistent and realistic? Are you convinced that the organisation's activities and services will actually contribute to the achievement of these objectives?

Service/activity targets
Does the business plan set clear service targets? Do you believe that these targets can be reached in the timescales set in the plan?

Environment

Does the plan have a clear and realistic understanding of the organisation's environment? Are you convinced that the information used to support the plan is both accurate and comprehensive?

SWOT analysis

Are you clear what the organisation's strengths and weaknesses are? Does the plan fail to identify any important opportunities for, or threats to, the organisation?

Marketing

Does the plan show an understanding of the contribution that marketing can make to achieving the organisation's objectives? How clear are the organisation's marketing objectives? Are you convinced that the organisation has identified the necessary marketing tools and resources to achieve these objectives?

Operations

Does the organisation have the people, equipment and systems to ensure that it can work effectively? Do you believe that the organisation understands the importance of service quality and has the means to ensure it? Are all the important operational issues covered in the plan?

Staffing and management

Are you convinced that the organisation has, or plans to develop, the staffing and management arrangements necessary to implement the business plan? How well do you think it will tap the skills and experience of volunteers and members of its management committee?

Finance

How realistic are the financial projections made in the business plan? Will the organisation have enough money to achieve its objectives? Has the organisation anticipated how it will respond to a shortage of money or to a cash flow crisis? Does the organisation have the financial management systems to monitor and control its finances?

Implementation

Does the organisatioin have a clear plan for implementing the business plan? Has it anticipated the implementation problems it will face and how it will deal with these problems?

Appendices

Do the appendices to the business plan contain sufficient information in support of the business plan?

2 *to identify any claims or assumptions in the plan that you feel need to be confirmed or verified.* Assumptions that may need further examination will include assumptions about

- the influence of environmental trends on the organisation;

- the needs of current and potential users of the services of the organisation; and

- the policies of funders and the likelihood of the organisation receiving the financial support it needs.

The actual verification of assumptions made in the business plan forms the third stage of your evaluation.

3 *to assess the extent to which the plan meets the presentation objectives discussed in Chapter 9.* You should judge the business plan against each of the six presentation objectives and make a note of any improvements you would like to see in the presentation of the plan.

Verification of claims and assumptions

It is not possible to prepare a business plan without making numerous claims and assumptions about an organisation, its services and its users. The strength of a business plan will, therefore, depend to a large degree on the accuracy and credibility of the assumptions made in it. There are several ways in which you can test or verify the assumptions in a business plan:

- by interviewing the people responsible for preparing the plan (focus on understanding why they reached the conclusions contained within the plan);

- by asking for additional information in support of assumptions made in the plan;

- by talking to a sample of the organisation's users to assess claims about user needs and satisfaction;

- by conducting further desk research into the conditions facing the organisation; and

- by interviewing those organisations and individuals whose financial support is essential to the success of the organisation. You may want to establish whether financial support included in the organisation's financial projections will actually be forthcoming.

Final assessment of the plan

Your final assessment of a business plan should include the following:

- a summary of your observations on the evaluation checklist;

- an assessment of the accuracy and credibility of key assumptions made in the business plan;

- recommendations on any revisions and additions, together with any changes in presentation, that you believe will improve the quality of the business plan.

Appendix 3

An A–Z of Business Planning Terms

A

Activity records   Forms on which staff detail the time they have spent on different activities. Completed weekly or monthly, activity records allow the monitoring of staff time and identify activities that need more resources.

Advertising   The presentation or promotion of ideas, services or products. Includes leaflets, posters and display signs. An important marketing tool.

B

Budgets   Prepared estimates of future financial events. Budgets can be prepared for income and expenditure, cash flow, marketing and individual service activities.

Business planning   The activity of preparing your organisation for events that will influence its future.

C

Capacity management   Involves estimation of the amount of staff resources you have to deliver your services and the organisation of your activities to reflect available resources.

Cash flow forecast   An estimate of the timing of your income and expenditure that will help you identify the cash needs of your organisation.

Contribution   A measure of the difference between the income and costs of a particular activity, eg a training course. It is common to talk of the contribution made by different activities to the core costs of an organisation.

Cost-benefit analysis A way of comparing the costs (money, time, etc) and benefits (increased effectiveness, user satisfaction, etc) of decisions, eg to invest in a desk top publishing system.

Cost centres Individual activities or sections of your organisation, eg training or publications, for which income and expenditure are separately identifiable. The major benefit of reporting financial information by cost centres is being able to see the financial contribution of each activity to the organisation.

D

Distribution The many ways in which you get your services to your users. Includes transport, premises and forms of communication such as mailings.

E

Environmental analysis The investigation and analysis of the world in which your organisation operates. Involves consideration of the effect on your organisation of government legislation, user needs, funding policies and the activities of other organisations.

Evaluation An assessment of the value or worth of an activity. It involves the measurement of performance and learning from experience.

F

Financial projections Estimates of income and expenditure and cash flow for the period covered by the business plan.

Focus groups A gathering of interested people to discuss a specific service or facility. An important way to collect original 'market research' information.

G

Goals Particular targets for each of the objectives of your organisation, eg 20 new members of a community centre.

H

Human resources The people you will work with to deliver your services. Includes staff, volunteers, management committee members and outside advisers.

I

Information Data or facts that are useful to your organisation. To be useful information should be relevant to your needs, up-to-date and comprehensive.

J

Job description A list of the responsibilities of an individual member of staff. Will usually indicate to whom the individual is accountable.

K

Key factors Those factors, eg people, expertise, etc, that are essential for success in a given activity.

L

Legal issues Issues affecting the legal structure or the constitution of your organisation, eg whether to establish a separate trading company.

M

Management information systems Systems for providing you with the information to make decisions and control the activities of your organisation. Includes activity and personnel records, enquiries, and financial information.

Marketing The process of matching your services to the needs of current and potential users.

Marketing information Information that you use to plan and monitor your marketing activity. Includes internal records, eg on service take-up, market intelligence and market research.

Marketing mix The range of marketing tools available to your organisation in conducting its marketing activity.

Monitoring The collection and analysis of 'factual' information, eg on the use of services, financial performance, etc.

N

Negotiation A process in which two or more individuals or organisations attempt to reach an agreement, eg on a contract for a service, on salary levels, etc.

O

Objectives The aims to which the activity of your organisation is directed. Your objectives describe what you hope to achieve by joining together and organising.

Outcomes The results or consequences of providing a service, eg a lower level of drug misuse as a result of an education campaign aimed at local schools.

Outputs Measures of the amount of service or activity you have delivered, eg number of counselling sessions provided.

Overhead costs Costs incurred by your organisation that are not attributable to any particular activity. Examples of overhead costs include rent and rates, insurance and administration.

P

Place A term used to describe marketing activity that is aimed at improving access to your services. It includes the location, accessibility and appearance of your premises.

Positioning statement A general statement of how your organisation plans to meet the needs of different groups of users. Some examples of positioning statements are provided in Chapter 5.

Price   A term used to describe marketing decisions on the charges you make for your services. It includes policies on discounts, arrangements for giving credit and pricing levels.

Primary research   Research designed to develop new or original information that is specific to the needs of your own organisation. Techniques include user surveys, focus groups and visits to exhibitions.

Process   The methods used to provide a service. It includes the policies and procedures of your organisation, eg an agreed procedure for assessing client needs.

Product   A term used in marketing to describe the content and range of the products and services you will use to meet user needs.

Promotion   Describes a range of marketing tools that include advertising, press and public relations and personal selling.

Q

Quality assurance   The ways in which you plan to ensure that your services have a high quality. Includes service standards, monitoring and evaluation and the collection of information on the effect of your services on the lives of users.

Questionnaires   Structured lists of questions designed to develop information, eg on the needs and views of your users. Questionnaires can be completed in person, by post or over the telephone. Some guidelines for preparing questionnaires are provided in Chapter 4.

R

Results   (see Outcomes).

Roles   The jobs, tasks or responsibilities of an individual, team or committee, eg marketing, financial management, etc.

S

Secondary research The study of published information such as publications, publicity produced by other organisations and information held by libraries. Also known as desk research.

Segmentation analysis The grouping of users according to shared characteristics, eg age, ethnicity, service usage and gender. An important task when preparing a marketing strategy.

Sensitivity analysis Involves measuring the effect of altering an important assumption, eg about the impact of changes in grant income on your organisation.

Staff turnover A measure of the extent to which your staff are leaving your organisation. Some staff turnover is inevitable but high rates of staff turnover can be both costly and disruptive.

SWOT analysis An analysis of the strengths and weaknesses of your organisation, and an assessment of its opportunities and threats.

T

Training Activities that improve the skills and confidence of staff, managers and volunteers. Includes courses, placements and distance learning.

U

Users The individuals and organisations that benefit from your activities. Also referred to as clients or customers.

V

Variance The difference between actual income and expenditure, and budgeted income and expenditure. A term used in financial management reports.

W

Weaknesses Activities or tasks that your organisation is not good at and that put your organisation at a disadvantage.

Z

Zero-based budgeting   A form of budgeting in which expenditure is estimated as if the organisation is being started for the first time. It involves a reassessment of the best way to allocate money in order to achieve objectives. Should be contrasted to budgets that take the previous year's figures as the starting point for financial projections.

Appendix 4

Useful Addresses and Publications

Case study organisations

The organisations featured in case studies and examples can be contacted at the following addresses:

Bromley Alcohol Advisory Service
171B High Street
Beckenham BR3 1AH
Tel: 081–663 6883

Charities Evaluation Services
Number One Motley Avenue
Christina Street
London EC2A 4SU
Tel: 071–613 1202
Fax: 071–613 0983
The organisation also has offices in Belfast, Exeter and Wales.

Child Accident Prevention Trust
4th Floor
Clerks Court
18–20 Farringdon Lane
London EC1R 3AU
Tel: 071–608 3828
Fax: 071–608 3674

Disability Resource Team
Bedford House
125–133 Camden High Street
London NW1 7JR
Tel: 071–482 5062
Fax: 071–482 0796

International Health Exchange
38 King Street
London WC2E 8JS
Tel: 071–836 5833
Fax: 071–379 1239

Language Line
18 Victoria Park Square
London E2 9PB
Tel: 081–983 4042
Fax: 081–981 6719

Voluntary Service Overseas
317 Putney Bridge Road
London SW15 2PN
Tel: 081–780 2266
Fax: 081–780 1326
The residential training centre
for which VSO conducted
market research (see Chapter 4)
will open during 1993.

Workable
Room CO5
Victoria House
98 Victoria Street
London SW1E 5JL
Tel: 071–915 0054
Fax: 071–630 9096

Four examples featured as case studies – Community Video Project, Downing Advice Centre, the Interpreters' Co-operative and the occupational therapy project – are all based on real organisations. The experience of the groups has been slightly amended and the true identity of the groups concealed.

Consultants

The Management Development Team at NCVO maintains a list of suitable consultants and trainers. It can be contacted at

NCVO
Regent's Wharf
8 All Saints Street
London N1 9RL
Tel: 071–713 6161
Fax: 071–713 6300

Nicholas Martin and Caroline Smith work for MBM Consulting Limited, 90 Woodstock Road, London N4 3EX Tel: 071–263 5560

References

The following publications were referred to in the text of the book.

Home Office, *Efficiency Scrutiny of Government Funding of the Voluntary Sector*, HMSO, 1990.

Lawrie, A., *Quality of Service. Measuring Performance for Voluntary Organisations*, NCVO/Directory of Social Change, 1992.

Lovelock, C.H. and Weinberg, C.B., *Public and Nonprofit Marketing*, The Scientific Press, 1989.

Further reading

Many books have been written to help private companies with business planning and you may wish to compare them with this book. Two such books are

Barrow, C., Barrow, P. and Brown, R., *The Business Plan Workbook*, Kogan Page, 1992.

West, C., *A Business Plan*, Pitman/NatWest Small Business Bookshelf, 1988.

For a more detailed discussion of market research techniques you will find the following a useful guide.

Crouch, S., *Marketing Research for Managers*, Pan Books, 1984.

An interesting book on developing an outcome-centred approach to funding has just been published and is available from NCVO. It suggests ways of developing outcome measures appropriate to voluntary organisations and recommends the preparation of business plans. The details of the book are

Williams, H.S. and Webb, A.Y., *Outcome Funding. A New Approach to Public Sector Grantmaking*, The Rensselaerville Institute, 1992.

Another book in the Pitman/NatWest Small Business Bookshelf provides useful information on employment and the law. The reference is

Lanz, K. *Hiring and Firing. Employing and Managing People*, Pitman/NatWest Small Business Bookshelf, 1988.

You can also obtain useful guidance notes and publications on this subject from the Advisory Conciliation and Arbitration Service (ACAS) at

Clifton House
83 Euston Road
London NW1
Tel: 071–388 5100

The development of the contract culture has increased the attention paid to costing services. NCVO and the Directory of Social Change have recently published an introductory guide to costing which you may find helpful.

Callaghan, J., *Costing for Contracts. A Practical Guide for Voluntary Organisations*, NCVO/Directory of Social Change, 1992.

Appendix 5

Names of People Whose Organisations Are Featured (for addresses see Appendix 4).

Trevor Groom
Director
Bromley Alcohol Advisory Service

Libby Cooper
Director
Charities Evaluation Services

Louise Pankhurst
Director
Child Accident Prevention Trust

Martin Coleman
Deputy Director
Disability Resource Team

Isobel McConnan
Director
International Health Exchange

Marc Kiddle
Director
Language Line

Brian Rockcliffe
Head of Operations
Voluntary Service Overseas

Heather Murison
Director
Workable

Index